MCSE Test Success:
Systems Management
Server 2

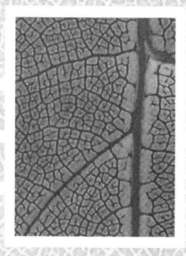

MCSE Test Success™:
Systems Management
Server 2

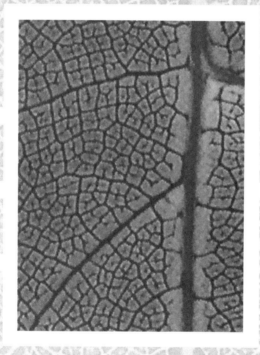

David G. Schaer

San Francisco • Paris • Düsseldorf • Soest • London

Associate Publisher: Guy Hart-Davis
Contracts and Licensing Manager: Kristine O'Callaghan
Acquisitions & Developmental Editor: Brenda Frink
Editor: Ann Houska
Project Editors: Lisa Duran, Bronwyn Shone Erickson
Technical Editor: John Friedrich
Book Designer: Bill Gibson
Graphic Illustrator: Tony Jonick
Electronic Publishing Specialist: Grey Magauran
Project Team Leader: Teresa Trego
Proofreader: Camera Obscura
Indexer: Matthew Spence
Cover Designer: Archer Design
Cover Illustrator/Photographer: FPG International

Library of Congress Card Number: 99-63316
ISBN: 0-7821-2368-6

Manufactured in the United States of America

10 9 8 7 6 5 4 3 2 1

For Josie and Morgan

Acknowledgments

Without the help and support of several people this book would never have happened. I'd like to thank Guy Hart-Davis, Bonnie Bills, and Brenda Frink for getting me involved in the project, Bronwyn Shone Erickson and Lisa Duran for coordinating the process, John Friedrich for his technical editing, and especially Ann Houska for putting all the right words in order. Teresa Trego, Grey Magauran, Camera Obscura, and Carl Montgomery all made contributions to turn this book into a final product.

Also, special thanks to Wally Mead and Janet Sheperdigian for squeezing me into the preview class, and to David Bowie, *Nick-at-Nite*, and Cafe du Monde coffee for helping me with the late nights.

Most of all I'd like to acknowledge my wife Josie and daughter Morgan for their support in all things, including this book.

Contents at a Glance

Table of Contents

Introduction

One of the greatest challenges facing corporate America today is finding people who are qualified to manage corporate computer networks. Many companies have Microsoft networks, which run Windows 95, Windows NT, and other Microsoft BackOffice products (such as Microsoft SQL Server and Systems Management Server).

Microsoft developed its Microsoft certification program to certify those people who have the skills to work with Microsoft products and networks. The most highly coveted certification is MCSE, or Microsoft Certified Systems Engineer.

Why become an MCSE? The main benefits are that you will have much greater earning potential and that an MSCE carries high industry recognition. Certification can be your key to a new job or a higher salary—or both.

So what's stopping you? If it's because you don't know what to expect from the tests or you are worried that you might not pass, then this book is for you.

Your Key to Passing Exam 70-086

This book provides you with the key to passing Exam 70-086, Implementing and Supporting Microsoft Systems Management Server 2. Inside, you'll find *all* the information relevant to this exam, including hundreds of practice questions, all designed to make sure that when you take the real exam, you are ready for even the most particular questions.

Understand the Exam Objectives

In order to help you prepare for certification exams, Microsoft provides a list of exam objectives for each test. This book is structured according to the objectives for Exam 70-086, designed to measure your ability to design, administer, and troubleshoot Microsoft networks.

At-a-glance review sections and more than 400 study questions bolster your knowledge of the information relevant to each objective and the exam itself. You learn exactly what you need to know without wasting time on background material or detailed explanations.

This book prepares you for the exam in the shortest amount of time possible—although to be ready for the real world, you need to study the subject in much greater depth and get a good deal of hands-on practice.

Get Ready for the Real Thing

More than 200 sample test questions prepare you for the test-taking experience. These are multiple-choice questions that resemble actual exam questions—some are even more difficult than what you'll find on the exam. If you can pass the Sample Tests at the end of each unit and the Final Review at the end of the book, you'll know you're ready.

Is This Book for You?

This book is intended for those who already have experience with SMS 2. It is especially well-suited for:

- Students using courseware or taking a course to prepare for the exam, and who need to supplement their study material with test-based practice questions.

- Network engineers who have worked with the product but want to make sure there are no gaps in their knowledge.

- Anyone who has studied for the exam—by using self-study guides, by participating in computer-based training, classes, or by getting on the job experience—and wants to make sure that they're adequately prepared.

Understanding Microsoft Certification

Microsoft offers several levels of certification for anyone who has or is pursuing a career as a network professional working with Microsoft products:

- Microsoft Certified Professional (MCP)
- Microsoft Certified Systems Engineer (MCSE)
- Microsoft Certified Professional + Internet
- Microsoft Certified Systems Engineer + Internet
- Microsoft Certified Trainer (MCT)

The one you choose depends on your area of expertise and your career goals.

Microsoft Certified Professional (MCP)

This certification is for individuals with expertise in one specific area. MCP certification is often a stepping stone to MCSE certification and allows you some benefits of Microsoft certification after just one exam.

By passing any certification exam that is current as of October 1, 1998—except for Networking Essentials—you become an MCP.

Microsoft Certified Systems Engineer (MCSE)

For network professionals, the MCSE certification requires commitment. You need to complete all of the steps required for certification. Passing the exams shows that you meet the high standards that Microsoft has set for MCSEs.

The following list applies to the NT 4 track. Microsoft still supports a track for 3.51, but 4 certification is more desirable because it is the current operating system.

To become an MCSE, you must pass a series of six exams:

1. Networking Essentials (waived for Novell CNEs)

2. Implementing and Supporting Microsoft Windows NT Workstation 4 (*or* Implementing and Supporting Windows 95 *or* Implementing and Supporting Windows 98)

3. Implementing and Supporting Microsoft Windows NT Server 4

4. Implementing and Supporting Microsoft Windows NT Server 4 in the Enterprise

5. Elective

6. Elective

Some of the electives include:

- Internetworking with Microsoft TCP/IP on Microsoft Windows NT 4

- Implementing and Supporting Microsoft Internet Information Server 4

- Implementing and Supporting Microsoft Exchange Server 5.5

- Implementing and Supporting Microsoft SNA Server 4

- Implementing and Supporting Microsoft Systems Management Server 2

- Implementing a Database Design on Microsoft SQL Server 6.5

- System Administration for Microsoft SQL Server 6.5

- Implementing and Supporting Microsoft Proxy Server 2

- Implementing and Supporting Microsoft Internet Explorer 4 by Using the Microsoft Internet Explorer Administration Kit

Microsoft Certified Systems Engineer (MCSE) + Internet

One of the newest certification designations is MCSE + Internet. This certification allows you to show that you have completed additional exams that qualify you as an Internet specialist.

For MCSE + Internet certification, you must pass a series of seven required exams:

1. Networking Essentials (waived for Novell CNEs)

2. Internetworking with Microsoft TCP/IP on Windows NT 4

3. Implementing and Supporting Microsoft Windows NT Workstation 4 (*or* Implementing and Supporting Windows 95 *or* Implementing and Supporting Windows 98)

4. Implementing and Supporting Microsoft Windows NT Server 4

5. Implementing and Supporting Microsoft Windows NT Server 4 in the Enterprise

6. Implementing and Supporting Microsoft Internet Information Server 4

7. Implementing and Supporting Microsoft Internet Explorer 4 by Using the Internet Explorer Administration Kit

You must also pass two elective exams. You can choose from:

- System Administration for Microsoft SQL Server 6.5

- Implementing a Database Design on Microsoft SQL Server 6.5

- Implementing and Supporting Web Sites Using Microsoft Site Server 3

- Implementing and Supporting Microsoft Exchange Server 5.5 (can also use version 5 exam)

- Implementing and Supporting Microsoft Proxy Server 2 (can also use version 1 exam)

- Implementing and Supporting Microsoft SNA Server 4

Microsoft Certified Trainer (MCT)

As an MCT, you can deliver Microsoft certified courseware through official Microsoft channels.

The MCT certification is more costly, because in addition to passing the exams, it requires that you sit through the official Microsoft courses. You also need to submit an application that must be approved by Microsoft. The number of exams you are required to pass depends on the number of courses you want to teach.

For the most up-to-date certification information, visit Microsoft's Web site at www.microsoft.com/train_cert.

Preparing for the MCSE Exams

To prepare for the MCSE certification exams, you should try to work with the product as much as possible. In addition, there are a variety of resources from which you can learn about the products and exams:

- You can take instructor-led courses.

- Online training is an alternative to instructor-led courses. This is a useful option for people who cannot find any courses in their area or who do not have the time to attend classes.

- If you prefer to use a book to help you prepare for the MCSE tests, you can choose from a wide variety of publications. These range from complete study guides (such as the books in the Network Press *MCSE Study Guide* series, which cover the core MCSE exams and most electives) to test-preparedness books similar to this one.

After you have completed your courses, training, or study guides, you'll find the *MSCE Test Success* books an excellent resource for making sure that you are prepared for the tests. With each of these books, you will discover if you've got the exam covered or if you still need to fill in some holes.

For more MCSE information, point your browser to the Sybex Web site, where you'll find certification information and descriptions of other quality titles in the Network Press line of MCSE-related books. Go to http://www.sybex.com.

Scheduling and Taking an Exam

Once you think you are ready to take an exam, call Prometric Testing Centers at (800) 755-EXAM (755-3926). They'll tell you where to find the closest testing center. Before you call, get out your credit card because each exam costs $100. (If you've used this book to prepare yourself thoroughly, chances are you'll only have to shell out that $100 once!)

You can schedule the exam for a time that is convenient for you. The exams are downloaded from Prometric to the testing center, and you show up at your scheduled time and take the exam on a computer.

Once you complete the exam, you will know right away whether you have passed or not. At the end of the exam, you will receive a score report. It will list the six areas that you were tested on and how you performed. If you pass the exam, you don't need to do anything else—Prometric uploads the test results to Microsoft. If you don't pass, it's another $100 to schedule the exam again. But at least you will know from the score report where you did poorly, so you can study that particular information more carefully.

Test-Taking Hints

If you know what to expect, your chances of passing the exam will be much greater. The following are some tips that can help you achieve success.

Get There Early and Be Prepared This is your last chance to review. Bring your Test Success book and review any areas you feel unsure of. If you need a quick drink of water or a visit to the restroom, take the time before the exam. Once your exam starts, it will not be paused for these needs.

When you arrive for your exam, you will be asked to present two forms of ID. You will also be asked to sign a piece of paper verifying that you understand the testing rules (for example, the rule that says that you will not cheat on the exam).

Before you start the exam, you will have an opportunity to take a practice exam. It is not related to Windows NT and is simply offered so that you will have a feel for the exam-taking process.

What You Can and Can't Take in with You These are closed-book exams. The only thing that you can take in is scratch paper provided by the testing center. Use this paper as much as possible to diagram the questions. Many times diagramming questions will help make the answer clear. You will have to give this paper back to the test administrator at the end of the exam.

Many testing centers are very strict about what you can take into the testing room. Some centers will not even allow you to bring in items like a zipped up purse. If you feel tempted to take in any outside material beware that many testing centers use monitoring devices such as video and audio equipment (so don't swear, even if you are alone in the room!).

Prometric Testing Centers take the test taking process and the test validation very seriously.

Test Approach   As you take the test, if you know the answer to a question, fill it in and move on. If you're not sure of the answer, mark your best guess, then "mark" the question.

At the end of the exam, you can review the questions. Depending on the amount of time remaining, you can then view all of the questions again, or you can view only the questions that you were unsure of. I always like to double-check all of my answers, just in case I misread any of the questions on the first pass. (Sometimes half of the battle is in trying to figure out exactly what the question is asking you.) Also, sometimes I find that a related question provides a clue for a question that I was unsure of.

Be sure to answer all questions. Unanswered questions are scored as incorrect and will count against you. Also, make sure that you keep an eye on the remaining time so that you can pace yourself accordingly.

If you do not pass the exam, note everything that you can remember while the exam is still fresh on your mind. This will help you prepare for your next try. Although the next exam will not be exactly the same, the questions will be similar, and you don't want to make the same mistakes again.

After You Become Certified

Once you become an MCSE, Microsoft kicks in some goodies, including:

- A one-year subscription to Microsoft Technet, a valuable CD collection that contains Microsoft support information.

- A one-year subscription to the Microsoft Beta Evaluation program, which is a great way to get your hands on new software. Be the first kid on the block to play with new and upcoming software.

- Access to a secured area of the Microsoft Web site that provides technical support and product information. This certification benefit is also available for MCP certification.

- Permission to use the Microsoft Certified Professional logos (each certification has its own logo), which look great on letterhead and business cards.

- An MCP certificate (you will get a certificate for each level of certification you reach), suitable for framing, or sending copies to Mom.

- A one-year subscription to *Microsoft Certified Professional Magazine*, which provides information on professional and career development.

How to Use This Book

This book is designed to help you prepare for the MCSE exam. It reviews each objective and relevant test-taking information, and offers you a chance to test your knowledge through study questions and sample tests.

The first six units in this book correspond to the Microsoft objectives groupings: Planning, Installation and Configuration, Configuring and Managing Resources, Integration and Interoperability, Monitoring and Optimization, and Troubleshooting. The seventh unit is a final review, which contains test questions pertaining to all the previous units.

For each unit:

1. Review the exam objectives list at the beginning of the unit. (You may want to check the Microsoft Train_Cert Web site to make sure the objectives haven't changed any since the book was published.)

2. Read through or scan the reference material that follows the objectives list. Broken down according to the objectives, this section helps you brush up on the information you need to know for the exam.

3. Review your knowledge in the Study Questions section. These are straightforward questions designed to test your knowledge of the topic. Answers to Study Questions are listed in the Appendix at the back of the book.

4. Once you feel sure of your knowledge of the area, take the Sample Test. The Sample Test's content and style matches the real exam. Set yourself a time limit based on the number of questions: A general rule is that you should be able to answer 20 questions in 30 minutes. When you've finished, check your answers with the Appendix in the back of the book. If you answer at least 85 percent of the questions correctly within the time limit (the first time you take the Sample Test), you're in good shape.

To really prepare, you should note the questions you miss and be able to score 95 to 100 percent correctly on subsequent tries.

5. After you successfully complete Units 1-6, you're ready for the Final Review in Unit 7. Allow yourself 90 minutes to complete the test of 55 questions. If you answer 85 percent of the questions correctly on the first try, you're well prepared. If not, go back and review your knowledge of the areas you struggled with, and take the test again.

6. Right before you take the test, scan the reference material at the beginning of each unit to refresh your memory.

At this point, you are well on your way to becoming certified!
Good Luck!

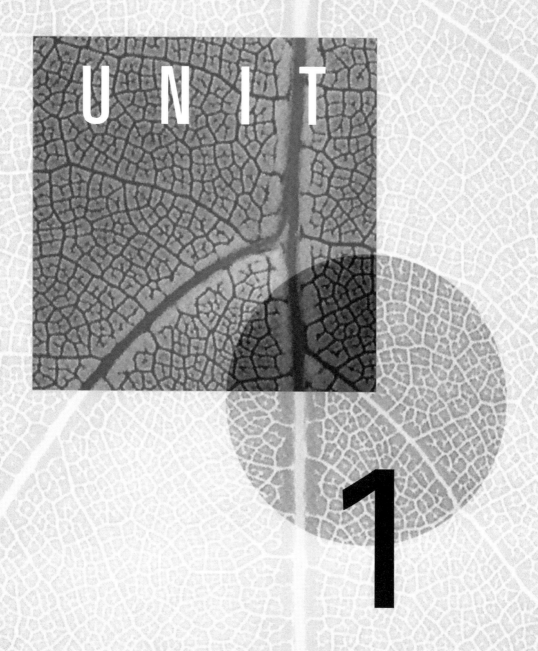

UNIT

1

Planning

Test Objectives

- **Design a Microsoft Systems Management Server (SMS) site; plan for various elements.**

  - Identify location of resources.

  - Identify types of resources, which consist of computers, printers, routers, users, and user groups.

  - Choose features of SMS to be implemented.

  - Identify hardware and software requirements for site systems.

- **Design an SMS site hierarchy.**

  - Identify the number of sites needed, based on considerations that include number and types of resources, network connectivity, and international issues such as language.

  - Identify the number of layers needed, based on considerations that include number and types of resources, network connectivity, and international issues such as language.

- **Plan a security strategy for SMS servers.**

  - Implement appropriate SMS accounts.

  - Implement access permissions for varying levels of SMS administration.

- **Plan the interoperability or upgrade for various situations.**

  - Plan the interoperability of a mixed SMS 1.2 and SMS 2 site.

  - Plan the upgrade of an SMS 1.2 site to an SMS 2 site.

Exam objectives are subject to change at any time without prior notice and at Microsoft's sole discretion. Please visit Microsoft's Training and Certification Web site (www.microsoft.com/Train_Cert/) for the most current listing of exam objectives.

Planning and design are the major factors contributing to a successful SMS installation or upgrade. This section includes, and expands on, the exam objectives as they relate to planning and design.

Key Features of SMS 2

As an integral part of the planning process, any organization must determine what goals it is trying to accomplish by using SMS 2. Obviously, the goals must be in line with the abilities and features of SMS. The following sections provide a brief overview of the key SMS 2 features you may choose to implement.

Hardware and Software Inventory

One of the key features of SMS 2 is its ability to maintain a hardware and software inventory for all systems throughout an organization. The information gathered by the clients is reported via the site server to a SQL database. An administrator can then perform queries against the database to determine which computers in the organization meet specific hardware criteria (e.g., memory, processor, and disk space), and which software is available on individual computers. This information can be used to generate *collections of resources* that meet specific criteria.

Software Distribution and Installation

These collections can then be used when targeting systems for the dissemination of software. For example, added to our test lab is a collection of NT 4 Workstations that haven't yet received NT Service Pack 3 (SP3) (see Figure 1.1). Let's consider how the queries against the SQL database can be used to populate a collection. Then we'll advertise NT SP3 to the collection and update the systems.

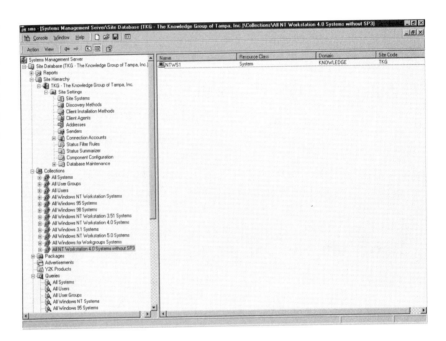

FIGURE 1.1

By viewing the collection, we can see that NTWS1 has not yet been updated with NT SP3.

Administrators don't need to be SQL gurus to extract meaningful information from the SQL Server. Using the SMS Administrator Console you can select from an extensive list of predefined queries and also create new queries by defining criteria using simple relational operators.

For example, the collection "All NT Workstation 4 Systems without SP3" is based on the query "All NT Workstation 4 Systems without SP3." By basing the collection on one or more queries, the collection can be kept updated automatically.

It is now possible for us to distribute NT Service Pack 3 to all members of the collection "All NT Workstation 4 Systems without SP3," by using the Distribute Software Wizard, as shown in Figure 1.2.

The availability of the software package is then advertised to members of the specified collection. The Advertised Program Client Agent, loaded on the client computer, monitors for the advertisement of new packages.

After installing the advertised package, clients report themselves as having NT Service Pack 3 installed. We can confirm the success of the package delivery and installation by checking the advertising status of the package, as shown in Figure 1.3.

FIGURE 1.2

The Distribute Software Wizard simplifies the distribution of software to a collection.

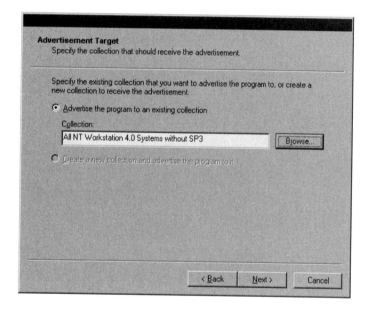

The reported inventory for the client will now reflect the updated service pack information (see Figure 1.4). When the collection "All NT Workstation 4 Systems without SP3" is updated based on the query, NTWS1 will be removed from the collection.

FIGURE 1.3

NT Service Pack 3 was
successfully installed
on NTWS1.

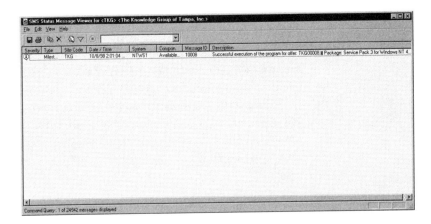

FIGURE 1.4

The updated
collection

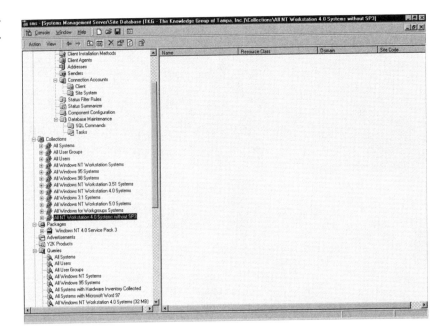

Software Metering

SMS 2 takes the control of software a step farther by incorporating software metering. With this utility you can control license restrictions from a central point. For example, if you own just three copies of a particular software package, you can restrict the number of concurrent copies that can be opened to three. With software metering you can also specify that particular applications can be run only during certain times of the day, by certain users or groups, and from specific computers.

Software metering can log the applications that are in use, by whom they are being used, and how long they have been in use. This information can help determine the necessity of purchasing additional licenses, the use of unauthorized software, and the charges that should be assigned to certain departments.

Remote System Support

The remote system support capabilities in SMS 2 allow you to perform most user support and system diagnostics remotely.

Both user support and system diagnostics can be performed from the SMS Administrator Console against any Microsoft Windows-based client version 3.*x* and greater.

As an example of the functionality, Figure 1.5 shows NTWS1 being remotely controlled from IRONMAN.

F I G U R E   1.5

NTWS1 is being controlled remotely from IRONMAN.

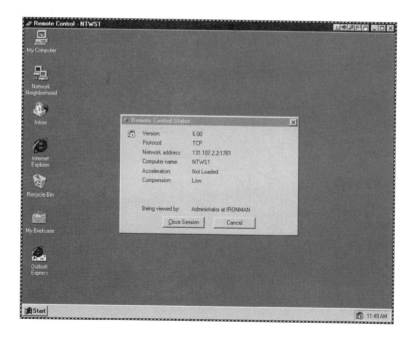

The Remote Tools available in SMS 2 for use with all Windows-based systems include the following:

- Remote Control
- Reboot
- Chat
- File Transfer
- Remote Execute
- Ping Test

When the focus of the Remote Tools is set to a Windows 3.x-based system, the following diagnostic tools also become available:

- Windows Memory
- Windows Modules
- Windows Tasks
- Windows Classes
- Windows Heap Walk
- GDI Heap Walk
- CMOS Info
- Device Drivers
- ROM Info
- Interrupt Vectors
- DOS Memory Map

Windows NT–based systems do not require access to the tools in the preceding list, as they provide information that is Windows 3.x specific or can be determined using the Windows NT Diagnostics tool. As shown in Figure 1.6, when the focus is set to a Windows NT–based system, the SMS Administrator Console calls the same Windows NT Diagnostics program that is available from administrative tools.

By using the Windows NT Diagnostics program, real-time system information can be collected unobtrusively.

FIGURE 1.6

The focus of the Windows NT Diagnostics program is set to the selected system.

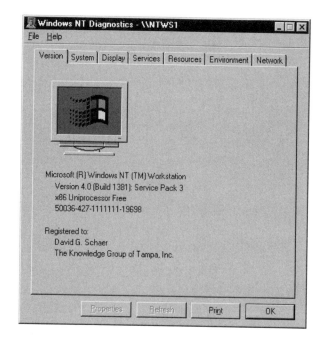

Network Mapping and Diagnostics

One of the most elusive areas of any organization's network is the physical network infrastructure. SMS 2 provides a means of documenting and diagnosing the physical network through a combination of reporting tools and diagnostic utilities.

Three different mechanisms are used in SMS 2 to help document and troubleshoot the physical network infrastructure:

- Network Discovery: Discovers and records information about the physical topology (routers, bridges, and the like), clients (IP address, computer name), and operating systems (operation system name, version).

- Network Trace: Offers a graphical depiction (see Figure 1.7) of the relationship among SMS site components using information gathered through Network Discovery.

F I G U R E   1.7

The test lab, as seen using Network Trace

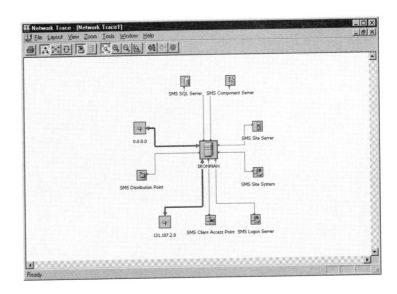

- Network Monitor: Gives administrators a simple, yet powerful software-based protocol analyzer. The SMS 2 Network Monitor includes "experts" that help to analyze data captured from the network.

Now that we've reviewed some of the basic functions of SMS 2, let's shift our attention to how certain terms are used in SMS 2.

SMS 2 Terminology

This section isn't intended to provide an exhaustive list of SMS 2 terms and definitions; we'll leave that to the glossary. However, it's important that you understand early on how certain terms are used and how they relate to each other within SMS 2.

Don't worry if you don't fully understand how each of the terms relates to one another at this point. At the end of this unit on planning, everything should be clear.

Some key SMS 2 terms to concentrate on are:

- Resource: Any computer, printer, router, hub, user account, group account, or other object that can be managed using SMS 2. For SMS 2 to identify a resource, the resource must first be discovered.

- Collection: Group of resources identified as a single entity; for example, "All Windows NT Workstation 4 Systems." The resources included in a collection may come from one or more sites. The primary purpose of creating collections is to simplify software distribution. Although membership in a collection can be explicitly assigned, it is normally better to maintain a collection through the use of queries.

- SMS Site: Primary or secondary site that contains all of the resources and site systems within boundaries defined by subnets. Depending on where the site is placed within the site hierarchy, the site will be the central site (the top-level parent site), a parent site, a child site, or both a parent and a child site. Each physical location within an organization is usually incorporated as a separate site.

- Primary site: An SMS site that has access to its own SQL database (not necessarily server). It is possible for two primary site servers to share the same SQL server. This may be done in a situation where a site is split in two primarily for administrative versus bandwidth issues. The primary site must record in the SQL database all information about resources in its sites and any sites below (child sites) in the SMS hierarchy.

- Secondary site: Because secondary sites do not have access to an SQL database, they are always child sites. Secondary sites are responsible for delivering information about their status and resources to their parent site. Because an SMS site should be created for each physical location, secondary sites provide a simple means of doing this for locations that don't have local administrators or SQL database access.

A secondary site cannot be upgraded to a primary site. It must be reinstalled as a primary site.

- Parent site: In the SMS hierarchy, a primary site responsible for recording resource and status information for both itself and one or more child sites.

- Child site: Primary or secondary site that reports its site information to a parent site. If the child site is a secondary site, then no additional child sites can exist below it. If the child site is a primary site, then it will also report information from its child sites to its parent.

- Central site: The primary site at the top of the SMS hierarchy. The central site's SQL database will contain the collective information received from all sites in the SMS site hierarchy.

- Sender: Means of managing the transfer of data among sites. Sender types include standard (LAN/WAN), remote access service (RAS) (ISDN, X.25, asynchronous, SNA), and Courier (e.g., CD-ROM sent via Federal Express). A sender must always be configured from a parent site to each of its child sites and from a child to its parent. A child site uses a sender to report information to its parent site. A parent site requires a sender to send packages and advertisements to a child site.

The Courier Sender is automatically created and configured and cannot be modified.

- Agent: Program run on the client computer to perform a specific SMS 2 action. For example, the Remote Tools Client Agent runs on the client to support remote control and diagnostic tools.

- Site server: A Windows NT Server (Windows NT Server 4, SP4 or above) with SMS 2 installed. If the site server is located in a primary site, it has the responsibility of recording collected information in a SQL database.

- Site system: Any system that performs a supporting role in SMS. For example, any system used as either a client access point (CAP) or a distribution point (DP) would be considered a site system. Specific details about each site system's function will be discussed in later chapters.

- Discovery: The process by which resources are identified. The discovery process is independent of the installation process.

Now that we've identified and defined some key SMS 2 terms let's consider the specific roles that site systems play. This will help you to better understand the correlation among the various objects.

Designing a Microsoft Systems Management Server (SMS) Site

Any major software implementation needs planning. The proper planning of your Microsoft Systems Management Server 2 (SMS 2), however, is a critical preparatory step, the importance of which cannot be overstated. Although SMS 2 is a versatile product that can be deployed to address a number of business concerns, it is not a cure-all for every network management issue. A single deployment plan is not sufficient to cover the nuances of each environment. The only true constants are the capabilities of SMS 2. Only by fully understanding what these capabilities are and how to implement them can you begin planning your deployment.

WARNING   SMS 1.*x* users, beware! Even though many SMS 2 concepts are the same in earlier SMS versions, their implementation in SMS 2 is vastly different.

This unit will introduce some basic SMS 2 features and help build your SMS 2 vocabulary. It will define the various resource elements available in SMS 2 and determine how to design an SMS 2 hierarchy. Later, the unit covers security issues and ends with a discussion on how to coexist with and upgrade from earlier versions of Microsoft Systems Management Server.

Identifying Location of Resources

According to SMS 2 terminology, a resource can include systems, user accounts, group accounts, printers, routers, and any SMS 2 manageable object. This broad definition of the word "resource" shows the diversity that SMS 2 is designed to accommodate. As administrators, we need to plan our sites with the understanding that the location and variety of resources will affect many decisions we make throughout each of the phases.

At this stage of your planning process you should already have a detailed physical plan of your existing network infrastructure (physical and logical); your objectives determined; and a clear understanding of the features of SMS 2 you will be implementing. Now by identifying the number and types of resources located throughout your organization, you can begin to determine your site requirements.

In SMS 2 site boundaries are based on subnets (either IP or IPX), whereas in SMS 1.*x* sites were composed of one or more domains. This new approach offers you excellent flexibility in design, deployment, and maintenance but also requires a detailed mapping of both the physical and the logical network.

Next you should obtain a detailed mapping of the physical and logical network, which should include at least the following:

Clients Hardware, software, and operating systems.

Servers Hardware, software, operating systems, location, primary function, and capacity.

Logical network Domains (number, trust relationships, active directory services, NDS configuration, bindery), and subnets (IP, IPX Network Numbers).

Physical network Segmentation, bandwidth, link capacity, traffic patterns, supported protocols, and server placement.

Security Account restrictions, account types, group usage, and methodology.

After detailing the physical and logical network, you are then ready to begin determining which resources you will be attempting to discover.

The types of resources that you will discover are determined by the discovery methods you implement. While the configuration of the discovery methods themselves is detailed in later chapters, it is important at this stage of the planning process to understand what resources can be discovered.

Identifying Types of Resources, Consisting of Computers, Printers, Routers, Users, and User Groups

The resources that can be discovered in SMS 2 are not limited to merely computers that can become SMS clients. In addition to computers, SMS resources can include printers, routers, users, and user groups. The resource types that can be located by each discovery method are listed here:

- Windows Networking Logon Discovery: computers (only those used by clients of configured NT domains)

- Windows NT User Account Discovery: NT Users (only NT global users extracted from the PDC of configured domains)

- Windows NT User Group Discovery: NT Groups (only NT global groups extracted from the PDC of configured domains)

- NetWare NDS Logon Discovery: computers (only those used by clients of configured NetWare 3.*x* servers)

- NetWare Bindery Logon Discovery: computers (only those used by clients of configured NetWare 4.*x* servers)

- Network Discovery: Any resources with an IP address including: computers, routers, printers, and other SNMP manageable devices.

The discovery of resources is one of the basic building blocks in establishing an SMS 2 site. The next section provides a high-level overview of each of the functions within SMS 2.

Choosing Features of SMS to Implement

Before considering the individual elements that define an SMS 2 site, it's a good idea to step back and consider the five basic capabilities of SMS 2, which address several network management issues:

- Hardware and software inventory: Determines the actual inventory of hardware and software within your enterprise.

- Software distribution and installation: Allows administrators to distribute and install software from a centralized location.

- Software metering: Monitors software licenses and usage throughout the enterprise.

- Remote system support: Enables the system to perform remote support and diagnostics.

- Network mapping and diagnostics: Generates details about your network infrastructure and troubleshoots network-related problems.

Even if you don't actually need all these features in your own implementation of SMS 2, you should become familiar with them. One of the major planning goals is to ensure that you "tread lightly" on the existing system, avoiding the creation of new problems during the implementation. Too often, administrators do not consider the consequences of a new deployment plan that incorporates every possible feature. SMS 2 is a large program and all of its capabilities may not be required at all locations within an organization. It is important to implement no more of the capabilities than are required, so as to avoid undue overhead expenses and unnecessary complications.

From the administrator's standpoint, most work will be done from within the Microsoft Management Console (MMC) version 1.1. The SMS Administrator Console, used to administer SMS 2, is provided as a snap-in to the MMC.

At this point in the book, let's see what the features of SMS 2 allow you to do, by looking at a simple SMS 2 site that is already installed and configured. The actual installation and configuration of the components will come later.

For "real-world" purposes, SMS 2 is designed to support environments with hundreds or even thousands of systems, but we'll be starting off with only two. Figure 1.8, showing the SMS Administrator Console being accessed from within the MMC, introduces us to our test lab.

FIGURE 1.8

Viewing the test lab from within the MMC

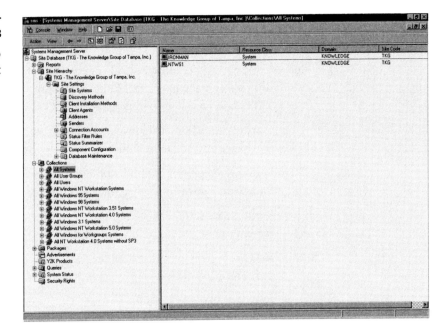

The test lab is initially configured with two computers: IRONMAN (NT Server 4, Service Pack 3) and NTWS1 (NT Workstation 4).

Note that the release version of SMS 2 requires NT Server 4 Service Pack 4 as a minimum.

Identifying Hardware and Software Requirements for Site Systems

In order to manage and control resources and the relationship between sites, SMS 2 relies on site systems to play one or more roles. Each role, as defined in the following table, provides some form of service to the SMS 2 system as a whole.

Four different objects can be assigned various site system roles: Windows NT servers, Windows NT shares, NDS volumes, and NetWare Bindery volumes. The object that is selected dictates the site system role(s) that can be performed.

Site System Role	Definition	Supporting Objects
SMS client access point (CAP)	A location used by clients to report their collected hardware and software information. Also the point from which clients are made aware of new advertisements and configuration changes. A CAP cannot be shared between sites.	Window NT server Windows NT share NetWare NDS volume NetWare Bindery volume
Component server (same as a helper server in SMS 1.2)	A server that runs various SMS 2 services instead of or in addition having the site server run them. Component servers are often used as a RAS sender when one is required and the site server does not have the capability I would list the components that can be added.	Window NT server
Distribution point	A location to which clients can attach in order to install advertised packages. No SMS components are installed on distribution points.	Window NT server Windows NT share NetWare NDS volume NetWare Bindery volume

Site System Role	Definition	Supporting Objects
Logon point	Location that provides the ability to use the various forms of logon discovery.	Windows NT server (controller with NTFS partition) NetWare NDS volume NetWare Bindery volume
Site database server	Runs Microsoft SQL Server and holds the actual site database.	Windows NT server
Software metering server	Hosts and maintains the software metering services.	Intel-based Windows NT server

It is not uncommon for a single server, like the one in our test lab, to play each of the different roles for a site. However, the location and types of resources are factors that help determine the optimal locations for the various roles to be assigned. For example, a network composed of both Microsoft Windows NT 4 clients and Novell NetWare 4.11 clients would likely require multiple client access points, distribution points, and logon points.

The following section will consider the part the location of resources plays in designing an SMS 2 system.

Designing an SMS Site Hierarchy

The next step in planning a functional SMS 2 installation is properly determining the SMS site hierarchy. The hierarchy establishes the logical relationship between distinct SMS sites and dictates where to report information.

Even though, in general, it is preferable to have as flat a hierarchy as possible, some specific considerations do need to be addressed.

Determining Resource Requirements

The number of resources that you determine must be supported both at present and in the future, as your organization grows. This is the first factor to consider when designing the hierarchy. Generally, the fewer the number of resources managed within a site, the better the site's performance will be.

Building a hierarchy is influenced by many internal and external factors. Even if we built our model in a vacuum, the following guidelines would still constrain us:

- Minimum recommended users or clients per site: 50; fewer would be considered wasteful of system resources.

- Maximum recommended clients per site: 10,000 to 30,000; this number may be substantially reduced by disabling some of the enabled features.

- Maximum number of layers supported: Unlimited; however, it is best to keep the hierarchy as flat as possible, with one, two, or three layers preferred.

- Maximum number of sites in a hierarchy: Limited by the number of unique three-character site codes available.

One rule of thumb is if you have 50 sites or more reporting to a single site, consider setting up another level in the hierarchy.

Although in many small organizations using SMS all of the users are located at the same physical location, it is more likely that groups of users will be spread across a wider geographic region. In this case, you must clearly identify the current and projected number of resources that SMS needs to manage at each physical location. This information will be key in determining each location's site server requirements. The number of users must also be considered in deciding when to divide a single location into multiple sites and when to combine multiple smaller groups into a single site.

Network Segmentation

The network you will be evaluating will probably have multiple segments, separated by a variety of devices. All of the resources located on the same physical LAN are usually members of the same site. Also, when a location has multiple segments with relatively few users on each segment, grouping the resources into a single site is often more cost effective than leaving them separate.

When the resources are separated, as in the case of a WAN, each location forms an individual site. This occurs even when a single domain spans multiple locations, or when controllers from the same site are located in many areas.

The major factors determining when to divide an organization into separate sites are the bandwidth capacity, availability, and requirements between the locations. Simply put, if only a slow link exists between locations you should consider splitting them into separate sites.

Having determined from your network segmentation map how you want to divide the network, you must now determine how sites will communicate.

Bandwidth Constraints

The bandwidth constraints between and sometimes within the locations now enter into the equation. It is necessary to ensure that a given location has the available bandwidth to support communication among the site server, the site systems, and the resources.

Communication between sites requires a sender, which can be configured to limit the amount of bandwidth used for intersite communication. You can even use the courier sender to transfer data offline among SMS 2 sites with limited bandwidth or no connectivity at all.

Although it may not be possible to fully quantify the bandwidth requirements, bandwidth is consumed by each of the following:

- Package distribution

- Software metering

- Resource reporting

- Resource discovery

- Administration

- Remote control, requiring 28.8kbps minimum

Recognizing that the available network bandwidth will be affected by various SMS-related factors, you should plan on deploying SMS 2 in a controlled manner. Using the information you gathered about the physical and logical networks, you can install and populate sites gradually by incorporating one subnet at a time. Be careful when discovering resources based on domain name, because a single domain may span multiple subnets and you might be generating more traffic and requiring more resources than intended.

Identifying the Number of Sites Needed

In the previous sections, we identified many reasons for dividing an organization into multiple sites. Let's now consider an example, to see how this works in practice.

Example Site Plan

The Example Company is an international company with offices in the following locations:

- Miami, Florida (Corporate Headquarters)
- Tampa, Florida
- Naples, Florida
- San Jose, Costa Rica (Latin American Headquarters)
- Caracas, Venezuela
- Frankfurt, Germany

Links among the company's locations, and IP subnet information, are shown in Figure 1.9.

FIGURE 1.9

The Example Company's network infrastructure

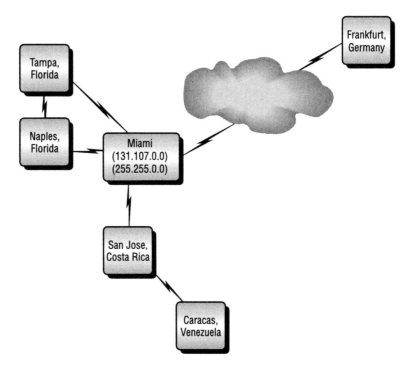

Based on the information provided in Figure 1.9 alone, it appears that Example Company should be divided into a minimum of six sites. Next, we need to consider the number of users at each location and any special administrative issues that might require any of the locations to be divided.

Once the division of the sites has been determined, we must next decide how the sites will communicate.

Identifying the Number of Layers Needed

Establishing relationships between individual SMS sites creates the SMS hierarchy. Although SMS 2 supports up to five layers in the hierarchy, it is preferable to use as few layers as possible. The flatter the hierarchy, the simpler the administration, configuration, and reconfiguration.

The Central Site

The site at the highest level in the hierarchy is called the central site. Its location depends on where the administrators of the overall network reside. All SMS information collected throughout the entire organization will be included in the central site's database. The central site is a form of parent site.

If a question does not provide enough information to determine conclusively where the central site should be located, it should be located at the corporate headquarters.

When properly designed, detailed information on each of the sites' resources should flow upstream to the central site, and administrators at each level should be able to manage their site and any sites below.

Parent Sites

Parent sites have the responsibility of maintaining collected information for both themselves and one or more child sites. The child sites may be either primary sites or secondary sites, but only primary sites can be parent sites.

Administrators located at a parent site have access to the information collected within their site and the details reported upstream to them from their child sites.

Child Sites

It might be said that the child site "chooses its parent" because the child site attaches itself to a primary site, making it a parent. A child site can have only one parent site; however, if its parent is also another site's child the information collected will flow "upstream." Eventually, all information gathered flows to the central site.

It is not uncommon to have an SMS installation where most of the sites are secondary sites, which are always child sites, reporting back to a single parent.

Example Hierarchy

Revisiting Example Company, we can see that the logical relationship between the locations does not necessarily correlate directly with the physical network infrastructure.

As shown in Figure 1.10, Miami has been chosen as the central site. Each of the sites, with the exception of Caracas, report directly to Miami. The Caracas site reports its information to San Jose, which reports to Miami; this makes the San Jose site both a child site and a parent site.

F I G U R E 1.10

Example Company's parent-child relationships

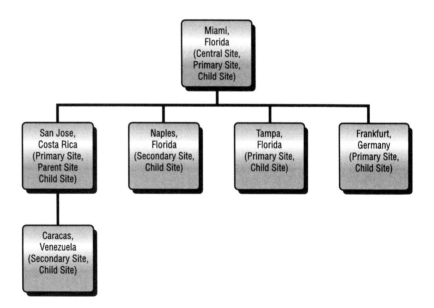

When actually implementing the hierarchy, the administrators will need to decide in which order to form the links between the sites. Sites can be added from the top-level of the hierarchy down or from the bottom-level up.

You should add sites from the lowest level and work toward the central site. This makes it easy to confirm that the proper information is being reported up the chain.

Additional Factors

There are a few additional hierarchy considerations to address while still in the planning stage. The determination of a hierarchy is usually a fairly straightforward process; however, it can be complicated when dealing with a global organization or when coexistence with an earlier version of SMS becomes an issue.

Globalization

SMS 2 is produced in different language versions, including U.S. English, German, and Japanese. Although you can use different language versions in the same hierarchy, some reported information will not get translated. For example, if the German version of SMS 2 will be used in Example Company's Frankfurt office, the administrators in Miami will need to be aware that status information reported from Frankfurt will show the message text in English and the insertion string in German.

Because the base-English character set is supported in the first half of all supported character sets, it is a good practice to use English characters for all network objects. This obviously won't address translation of reported information but will provide an underlying layer of consistency.

Preexisting SMS 1.2 Sites

Integration and coexistence deserve to have a whole heading devoted to them; in fact, that section is coming up soon. At this point, though, it is important to note that SMS 1.2 sites can report information to either SMS 2 sites or other SMS 1.2 sites. However, SMS 1.2 sites can support only child sites that are also running SMS 1.2.

Planning a Security Strategy for SMS Servers

While still in the planning stage, you need to consider how security will be implemented, both within and between sites. Proper planning will ensure that the SMS accounts can communicate and that administrators have the appropriate level of access to site objects.

This section addresses the function of each of the SMS accounts and how to establish proper administrative levels.

Implementing Appropriate SMS Accounts

During the installation of SMS 2, several site service accounts will be created. These accounts will be used to ensure that the SMS 2 services are able to perform their required functions in a secure manner.

Because the SMS 2 security is integrated with the Windows NT logon security, you might need to establish trust relationships between domains that are encompassed by the same site.

The site system accounts and their functions are listed in the table below.

Account	Function	Requirements
SMS Service Account (SMSService)	Used by the SMS site systems to communicate.	Membership in Administrators and the right to log on as a service on the site server.
SMS Remote Service Account (SMSsvc_*sitecode)*	Used by the Windows Networking Logon Discovery Agent to discover clients. A separate account is created for each CAP.	Membership in Domain Users and Administrators.
SMS Site Address Account	Used when transferring data between parent and child sites.	Change permissions to the target site's \SMS\inboxes\ despoolr\receive box.
SMS Logon Service Account (SMSLogonsvc)	Used by the logon discovery agent to copy discovered data to the site server.	Membership in Administrators, Domain Users, and the right to log on as a service.
SQL Server Account	Used by the site server to connect to the SQL server.	Standard or integrated security can be used. In either case, the account must have "sa" permissions at the SQL server.
SMS Site System Connection Account (SMSServer_*sitecode)*	Used to retrieve resource information from CAPs. Used by discovery agents to locate user and group accounts.	Membership in Domain Users within each domain where resources are being discovered.

Additional accounts are used to provide specific Windows NT client-side functions. Information on each of these accounts is provided in the following table.

Account	Function	Requirements
SMS Client Network Connection Account (SMSClient_*sitecode*)	Used by the client when connecting to CAPs and DPs	Read rights to CAPs and DPs.
SMS Client Software Installation Account	Used primarily during unattended installations; this account makes the success of the installation independent of the logged on user.	Administrative rights.
SMS Client Remote Installation Account	Used on NT clients when the logged on user does not have sufficient rights to install SMS client software.	Administrative rights to NT clients. Required for NT-based NetWare clients.
SMS Windows NT Client Remote Control Account	Used when attempting to remote control NT clients.	Membership in the permitted viewers list.

Most SMS account details are entered during installation. If you need to modify accounts after installation, this can be done using the SMS Administrator Console.

Implementing Access Permissions for Varying Levels of Administration

To properly assign administrator rights in SMS 2, you have to understand how the SQL Administrator Console uses Web-based Enterprise Management (WBEM).

WBEM represents a layer of components that acts as an intermediary between the SMS Administrator Console and the common information model (CIM) , which in turn interfaces with SQL Server. By using WBEM, all of the SMS objects can be controlled collectively by groups (classes) or as individual objects (instances).

Exposing the SMS 2 objects to the SMS Administrator Console allows the administrator to grant or deny rights to any of the objects. Rights can be assigned either to individual users or to groups of users.

The following table identifies the rights associated with various SMS 2 objects.

Object Type	Permissions
Advertisements	Delete, Modify, Read
Packages	Administer, Create, Delete, Distribute, Modify, Read
Collections	Administer, Advertise, Create, Delete, Delete Resource, Modify, Modify Resource, Read, Use Remote Tools
Queries	Administer, Create, Delete, Modify, Read
Sites	Administer, Create, Delete, Modify, Read
Status messages	Administer, Create, Delete, Read

Because rights to access and control objects are based on Windows NT accounts, you can follow the same basic methodology of placing accounts into global groups, making the global groups members of local groups, and finally assigning permissions to the local groups. By performing administration in this manner you can control object access based on group membership. For example, the security group may be granted the right to distribute an antivirus package. A person who is a member of this group would inherently have the same right. If the person were removed from the group, the associated privilege would be lost.

Planning for Interoperability and Upgrades

It is generally the rule, not the exception, that we have to accommodate preexisting systems in our installation plans. This section considers coexistence with and upgrading from previous versions of SMS.

Planning the Interoperability of a Mixed SMS 1.2 and SMS 2 Site

It may not be feasible to upgrade all sites from SMS 1.2 to SMS 2 immediately. Let's consider some of the times when it may be necessary or easier to integrate SMS 1.2 and SMS 2 sites.

SMS 1.2 sites should be maintained if any of the following conditions exist:

- Site contains Macintosh, MS-DOS, or OS/2 clients.
- Clients are using server-based applications with the Package Command Manager (PCM).
- OS/2-based LAN Manager site servers exist.

If SMS 1.2 sites must be maintained, you should consider the following:

- SMS 1.2 sites must fall below SMS 2 sites in the hierarchy.
- SMS 1.2 sites can be administered only using the SMS Administrator program.

Although SMS 1.2 and SMS 2 can be used together, you will probably want to upgrade when possible to SMS 2, in order to take advantage of its additional features.

Planning the Upgrade from an SMS 1.2 to an SMS 2 Site

Preparation and planning are essential for a successful upgrade of SMS versions. Although coexistence has already been discussed, coexistence and upgrading are not mutually exclusive. SMS 1.2 sites and SMS 2 sites must usually coexist while the older sites are being upgraded.

When upgrading from SMS 1.2 to SMS 2, observe the following guidelines:

- SMS 2 sites cannot exist below SMS 1.2 sites in the hierarchy, so upgrade sites from the central site down.
- Sites with unsupported clients cannot be upgraded, so separate the supported from the unsupported clients, and form a new site.
- Set the tempdf database of the server to 1.2 times the size of the existing SMS database.

- The SMS 1.2 directory will be deleted during the upgrade, so copy any packaged definition files or custom MIF files you want to upgrade to a separate directory.

WARNING   Make sure to move any objects you want to preserve during the upgrade from within the SMS 1.2 directory as it will be deleted during the upgrade process.

- Sites to be upgraded must run a minimum of SMS 1.2 with Service Pack 4. The SNA sender is no longer supported. Sites requiring connectivity via SNA should use the new SNS RAS sender.

Finally, before conversion, you should document as much as possible about the existing sites. Documentation will prove vital in ensuring that the upgrade is successful and that you have addressed all of the requirements.

Designing a Microsoft Systems Management Server (SMS) Site

1. True/False: SMS 2 provides a means of collecting both hardware and software inventory.

2. True/False: Using SMS 2, software distribution can be managed from a central location.

3. True/False: Software licensing can be monitored using the Network Monitor feature of SMS 2.

4. True/False: It is required to implement all features of SMS 2 in each connected site.

5. SMS 2 is administered using the Microsoft Management Console (MMC) version _____ and the SMS Administrator Console snap-in.

6. The collected inventory details are stored in a _____ database.

7. True/False: It is necessary to understand SQL syntax to perform queries using SMS 2.

8. To have a collection be maintained automatically it must be based on a _____.

9. Which SMS 2 feature lets you restrict the number of concurrent users of a given software package?

10. Remote system support is available only to _____-based clients.

11. Network _____ can be used to capture and analyze packets from the network.

12. Network _____ is used to learn specifics about the physical network infrastructure.

13. Network _____ provides a graphical depiction of the relationship between SMS 2 sites and components.

14. When used in SMS 2, _____ refers to any object that can be managed by using SMS 2.

15. When used in SMS 2, _____ refers to a grouping of resources.

16. An SMS 2 site's boundaries are defined by _____.

17. An SMS 2 site that is responsible for recording information directly into the SQL database on behalf of itself and other sites is both a _____ site and a _____ site.

18. True/False: Each physical location in an organization should generally be defined as a separate site.

19. A _____ site cannot record information directly to the SQL database.

20. True/False: Child sites are always secondary sites.

21. The _____ site is the site highest in the SMS 2 site hierarchy.

22.   Which SMS 2 component is responsible for the transfer of data between sites?

23.   What is the minimum version of Windows that must be installed on a site server?

24.   _____ sites are generally installed at locations without local administrators.

25.   True/False: A child site can never be a parent site.

26.   Where do SMS 2 clients receive advertisements from and report inventory information to?

27.   A _____ server runs various SMS 2 services instead of or in addition to the site server running them.

28.   Clients attach to _____ points to install advertised packages.

Designing an SMS Site Hierarchy

29.   True/False: The site hierarchy should be kept as flat as possible.

30.   The minimum recommended number of users per site is _____.

31.   The maximum recommended number of users per site is _____.

32.   The maximum number of layers supported in the SMS 2 hierarchy is _____.

33. True/False: All resources located on the same LAN are usually members of the same site.

34. True/False: When a single domain spans a WAN, all locations must be members of the same site.

35. True/False: When physical locations are connected by slow links, they should be incorporated as separate sites.

36. The _____ sender should be used between sites without direct connectivity.

37. True/False: The bandwidth utilization between sites can be governed on a per sender basis.

38. Remote control requires a minimum available bandwidth of _____kbps.

39. True/False: The central site's database includes all the SMS information collected throughout the entire organization.

40. True/False: The central site should be located at the physical center of the network infrastructure.

41. Only _____ sites can be parent sites.

42. True/False: A child site can have a maximum of five parent sites.

43. A parent site should have a maximum of _____ child sites directly reporting to it.

44. True/False: The site hierarchy should always correspond to the physical network infrastructure.

45. True/False: It is possible to use different language versions of SMS in the same hierarchy.

46. True/False: SMS 2 sites can coexist with SMS 1.2 sites in the same hierarchy.

47. True/False: SMS 1.2 sites can report information to either SMS 1.2 or SMS 2 sites.

48. True/False: SMS 2 sites can report information to either SMS 1.2 or SMS 2 sites.

Planning a Security Strategy for SMS Servers

49. What must you establish when implementing a site encompassing multiple domains?

50. The _____ account is used by SMS site systems to communicate.

51. The _____ account is used by the Windows Networking Logon Discovery Agent.

52. The _____ account is used by the site server to connect to the SQL server.

53. SQL Server can be configured to use either _____ or _____ security.

54.   True/False: To perform an unattended installation, the logged on user at the client computer must have local administrative rights.

55.   The _____ layer acts as an intermediary between the SMS Administrator Console and CIM.

56.   Rights to SMS objects can be controlled at the _____ or _____ levels.

Planning for Interoperability and Upgrades

57.   True/False: SMS 2 supports all of the features and client types as SMS 1.2.

58.   True/False: The SMS Administrator Console supports administration of both SMS 2 and SMS 1.2 sites.

SAMPLE TEST

1-1 Which of the following site system roles can be assigned to a Novell NetWare 4.11 server?

A. SMS client access point

B. Component server

C. Distribution point

D. Logon point

E. Software metering server

1-2 The administrator wants to ensure that the site server is not overburdened with services. She determines that it would be most effective to locate the RAS sender on a separate server.

Which of the following terms best describes the site system role performed by the server housing the RAS sender?

A. Distribution point

B. Component server

C. Logon point

D. SMS client access point

1-3 The Example Company has a total of 10,000 users, dispersed among three locations: Miami (4000), Tampa (3000), Orlando (3000).

Both Tampa and Orlando are connected to the headquarters in Miami via high-speed links.

The administrator has been asked to design a site hierarchy that meets the following objectives:

Required result: Allow administrators in Miami to distribute packages to systems at all locations.

Desired result: Maximize the performance of SMS at all sites.

Solution: The administrator recommends establishing three sites, based on physical location. Miami would act as the central site; Tampa and Orlando would be child sites.

Which of the following statements best describes the effectiveness of the administrator's plan?

    A. The solution meets both the required and the desired objectives.

    B. The solution meets only the required objective.

    C. The solution meets only the desired objective.

    D. The solution meets neither the required nor the desired objective.

1-4 The administrator of the Example Company has implemented the master domain model for account validation. The primary domain controller is located in Miami, and backup domain controllers are located in both Tampa and Orlando. The sites are connected via high-speed links.

The administrator has been asked the best way to implement resource discovery while meeting the following objectives:

Required result: Identify all SMS objects throughout the account and resource domains.

Desired result: Limit the amount of traffic generated on the network.

Solution: The administrator recommends performing resource discovery based on individual subnets.

How well does the administrator's solution meet the required and desired objectives?

    A. The solution meets both the required and the desired objectives.

    B. The solution meets only the required objective.

    C. The solution meets only the desired objective.

    D. The solution meets neither the required nor the desired objective.

1-5 The administrator of Example Company has established both Orlando and Tampa as child sites below Miami. After connecting the sites she notices that, although information from both sites is being reported to Miami, she cannot advertise packages to either location.

What is the most likely cause of the problem?

   A. Miami can support only a single child site.

   B. The administrator does not have sufficient rights in the child sites.

   C. Senders have not been configured from Miami to the child sites.

   D. Addresses for the child sites have not been created in Miami.

1-6   Which of the following statements regarding SMS 1.2 and SMS 2 integration are correct?

   A. SMS 1.2 sites can be parents to other SMS 1.2 sites.

   B. SMS 1.2 sites can be parents to SMS 2 sites.

   C. SMS 1.2 sites can only be child sites.

   D. SMS 2 sites can be parents to SMS 1.2 sites.

1-7   The administrator of Example Company's network wants to generate a graphic showing the relationships between the SMS site systems.

   Which one of the following tools should the administrator use to create the graphic?

   A. Network Monitor

   B. Performance Monitor

   C. Network Discovery

   D. Network Trace

1-8   Example Company has recently acquired a three-person firm in Tampa. Tampa is a secondary site that reports to Miami as its parent. The new company will be physically linked to Example Company's corporate network with a 128-kbps ISDN line.

   The administrator has been asked to incorporate the new company into the SMS system while meeting the following objectives:

   Required result: The administrators in Tampa must be able to manage all resources reported from the new company.

Desired result: All resources discovered in the new company should be reported upstream to the headquarters in Miami.

Solution: The administrator recommends making the new company a child site of the Tampa site.

How well does the administrator's solution meet the required and desired objectives?

- **A.** The solution meets both the required and the desired objectives.
- **B.** The solution meets only the required objective.
- **C.** The solution meets only the desired objective.
- **D.** The solution meets neither the required nor the desired objective.

1-9   Example Company has recently acquired a three-person firm in Tampa. Tampa is a secondary site that reports to Miami as its parent. The new company will be physically linked to Example Company's corporate network with a 128-kbps ISDN line.

The administrator has been asked to incorporate the new company into the SMS system while meeting the following objectives:

Required result: The administrators in Tampa must be able to manage all resources reported from the new company.

Desired result: All resources discovered in the new company should be reported upstream to the headquarters in Miami.

Solution: The administrator recommends including the new company's subnet within the boundaries of the Tampa site.

How well does the administrator's solution meet the required and desired objectives?

- **A.** The solution meets both the required and the desired objectives.
- **B.** The solution meets only the required objective.
- **C.** The solution meets only the desired objective.
- **D.** The solution meets neither the required nor the desired objective.

SAMPLE TEST

1-10 The administrator has created a global group named SMStechs and wants to assign it permission to manage the creation and distribution of packages throughout the site.

From where will the administrator assign the permissions to the SMStechs group?

    A. User Manager for Domains, Policies, User Rights

    B. WBEM

    C. SQL Security Manager, Security, Grant New

    D. SMS Administrator Console, SMS Server, Site Database, Security Rights

1-11 The employees of Example Company are allowed to browse the Internet during lunchtime. It is believed that some users are abusing the privilege by surfing during work hours and visiting inappropriate sites.

What is the most effective way of controlling the permitted access times and locations for the network users?

    A. Monitor the network, using Network Monitor.

    B. Install a proxy server.

    C. Use software metering to control valid access times.

    D. Track the locations being visited with Network Trace.

1-12 The administrator of Example Company's network needs to advertise and distribute packages to a collection of Novell NetWare 3.12 clients.

Which of the following system roles should be established using a NetWare Bindery volume?

    A. SMS client access point

    B. Component server

    C. Distribution point

    D. Logon point

SAMPLE TEST

1-13   Which of the following system roles can a Windows NT share be used to perform?

    A. SMS client access point

    B. Distribution point

    C. Logon point

    D. Software metering server

1-14   Which of the following statement about an SMS central site is correct?

    A. The central site is always a primary site.

    B. The central site is always located in the middle of the logical site hierarchy.

    C. The central site is always located in the middle of the physical network infrastructure.

    D. The central site must reside in a separate Windows NT domain.

1-15   The administrator of Example Company needs to distribute a large program update to a site that is located across a slow link.

Which of the following senders should the administrator use to distribute the package?

    A. Standard

    B. RAS with SNA

    C. RAS with X.25

    D. Courier

1-16   Which of the following senders exist in SMS 2 but were not included with SMS 1.2?

    A. RAS (SNA)

    B. SNA (batch)

    C. Courier

    D. RAS (ISDN)

SAMPLE TEST

1-17   Which of the following statements regarding parent sites are correct?

    A. Parent sites must be primary sites.

    B. Parent sites can also be child sites.

    C. Parent sites require addresses of their child sites in order to communicate with them.

    D. The central site can be a parent site.

1-18   Which of the following can be used to define site boundaries?

    A. NT domains

    B. AppleTalk zones

    C. IP subnets

    D. IPX network numbers

1-19   Which of the following are required for the SMS Service Account (SMSService) to properly communicate and transfer data between SMS site systems?

    A. Membership in the Users group.

    B. Membership in the Administrators group.

    C. The right to log on as a service.

    D. The right to act as part of the operating system.

1-20   Which of the following statements regarding primary sites are true?

    A. Each primary site requires its own SQL database.

    B. Each primary site requires its own SQL Server.

    C. Primary sites are always parent sites.

    D. A single primary site can have multiple child sites below it on the hierarchy.

UNIT

2

Installation and
Configuration

Test Objectives

- **Install, configure, and modify a primary site server.**
  - Use Express Setup and Custom Setup.
  - Configure the Microsoft Windows NT Server computer that will be the site server.
  - Set up Microsoft SQL Server during SMS Setup.
  - Use a remote SQL Server.
  - Shut down, reset, and restart the current installation.
  - Change the username and password of the SMS service account.
  - Change the SQL Server information.
  - Remove SMS.
  - Install new SMS components.

- **Install a secondary site server.**
  - Perform the installation from the CD-ROM.
  - Perform a network installation by using files from the network or the CD-ROM.

- **Configure site system roles.**
  - Configure component servers.
  - Configure logon points.
  - Configure distribution points.
  - Configure client access points.
  - Configure software metering servers.
  - Configure the SMS Administrator console.

- **Configure a site hierarchy.**
  - Configure site addresses.
  - Add and configure senders, which consist of Standard, Courier, and RAS.
  - Implement parent-child relationships.
  - Remove a site from the site hierarchy.

Exam objectives are subject to change at any time without prior notice and at Microsoft's sole discretion. Please visit Microsoft's Training and Certification Web site (www.microsoft.com/Train_Cert/) for the most current listing of exam objectives.

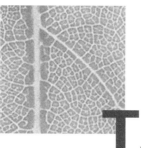

This unit will help you review the necessary steps involved in the installation and configuration of SMS 2 site servers and supporting systems.

Installing, Configuring, and Modifying a Primary Site Server

The following sections will consider the installation, configuration, and modification of a primary site server. First, however, it is important to review some of the basic characteristics of a primary site:

- Primary sites require a SQL Server database.

- Primary sites can be directly administered and generally have a dedicated administrator.

- Primary sites can be parent sites, child sites, or both.

The installation of a primary site begins with the configuration of the primary site server and its supporting SQL Server database. The exam will require that you be familiar with the installation requirements of the primary site server and of SQL Server, and with the configuration of the SQL Server database.

Using Express Setup and Custom Setup

Primary site servers can be installed using either the Express Setup or the Custom Setup method. The Express Setup is offered more as a convenience than as a real-world solution. The primary differences between the two methods are outlined here:

- Express Setup enables all installation and discovery methods, with the exception of Network Discovery. Custom Setup enables only installation and discovery methods selected.

- Although Express Setup enables all logon-based installation and discovery methods it does not enable the Modify Logon Scripts option. Express Setup installs and utilizes a copy of SQL Server locally on the primary site server. Custom Setup can direct the SQL Server database to either a local or a remote SQL Server.

- Express Setup installs all required and optional SMS components. Custom Setup installs by default only the primary site server components and the SMS Administrator Console.

- Express Setup is offered as an option only if a SQL Server is not installed on the proposed site server.

Custom Setup offers greater flexibility and freedom of choice in installation options. For example, using Custom Setup you can install SQL Server either locally or remotely and you can choose the specific components that will be installed and enabled.

Configuring the Microsoft Windows NT Server Computer That Will Be the Site Server

The site servers are key systems and as such deserve to be configured with significant memory and processing power. However, for purposes of the exam it is perhaps better to focus on the minimum requirements than on real-world recommendations.

The minimum hardware and software requirements for a site server running SMS 2 are as follows:

- Intel Pentium 133 or DEC Alpha processor

- 1GB of available hard disk space on a NTFS64–96MB of RAM (128MB recommended)

- Microsoft Internet Explorer 4.01 and Service Pack 1 (SP1) or later

- Microsoft Windows NT Server 4 with SP4 with Microsoft Data Access Components (MDAC) and Y2K components installed, or later

- Microsoft SQL 6.5 with SP5, or Microsoft SQL 7

Although it should go without saying, make sure that all of the equipment is listed on the hardware compatibility list (HCL).

SP 4, MDAC, Y2K components, and Microsoft Internet Explorer 4.01 and SP1 are automatically installed when you apply the service pack from the SMS installation compact disk.

Setting up Microsoft SQL Server during SMS Setup

During an Express Setup of a primary site you must perform the installation of Microsoft SQL Server 6.5 with SP5 or Microsoft SQL Server 7. The setup of either version of SQL Server is fairly straightforward. You need only supply the path to the SQL Server setup files and the appropriate CD-Key.

Express Setup will install the Microsoft SQL Server on the same system used as the primary site server using default settings for security mode, character set, and sort order.

Using a Remote SQL Server

At times it might be desirable to use a remote copy of SQL Server as opposed to one installed on the same machine as the site server. For example, if multiple sites are established for reasons of administration more than of bandwidth, it may be possible for two sites to share the same SQL Server. Also, if a company is already using SQL Server, it might be more cost effective to use it to house the SMS databases.

Extra care must be taken when using an existing SQL Server 6.5 to specify new or empty devices for holding the SMS database. Although existing devices can be used, any databases located on the devices will be dropped.

You can't assign a remote SQL Server when you use Express Setup. However, regardless of the setup method used, the SMS database can be relocated to another SQL Server after the installation is complete.

When a remote SQL Server is used, you have the option of running the SMS provider on the primary site server or on the SQL Server (see Figure 2.1). Generally, the SMS provider should run on the same machine as SQL Server, but it can be run on the site server if the additional workload degrades SQL Server performance for other applications.

FIGURE 2.1

Determining the
location of the
SMS provider

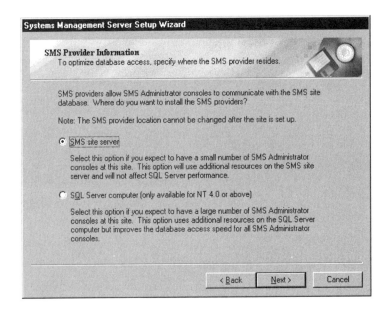

Shutting Down, Resetting, and Restarting the Current Installation

This exam objective deals with options available to an administrator running the SMS Setup program from the SMS program group. There are three specific things that can be performed by running the SMS Setup program: Changing the SMS Service Account, Changing SQL Server information, and Removing SMS. Each option is detailed in the next three sections.

Changing the Username and Password of the SMS Service Account

Modifying SMS service account information is simple. By running the Setup program from the SMS program group, you can either update the current account's password or specify a new SMS service account. If a new account is entered, SMS will verify, and rectify if necessary, that it is a member of Domain Admins and has the right to log on as a service.

Changing the SQL Server Information

You must keep the SMS primary site server aware of changes to the SQL Server configuration. It is necessary to run Setup from the SMS program group if any of the following items are changed:

- SQL logon account: The default is to use the "sa" account; however, it is possible to use any account that maps to "sa" or, as in the case of SQL 7, to use any account assigned the sysadmin role.

- Security mode: The default is to use standard security mode, but standard, integrated, or mixed modes can be used.

In SQL Server 7 the authentication mode choices are either "SQL Server or Windows NT" or "Windows NT only," which correspond to mixed and integrated, respectively.

- Database location: If the SMS database is moved to a different SQL Server, it is necessary to inform the primary site server of the new location.

Running the SMS Setup program cannot be used by itself to move the SMS database. The Setup program merely updates the primary site server's registry to include the new SQL Server information. The physical move of the SMS database must be performed using the SQL Server Enterprise Manager.

Removing SMS

You can remove primary and secondary sites by running SMS Setup. Any parent-child relationships between sites should be broken before beginning the removal of software.

Although you can remove secondary sites by running Setup from the SMS installation CD-ROM, it is preferable to remove these sites from within the SMS Administrator Console using the Delete Secondary Site Wizard.

When you delete SMS from a primary site server, you can elect to have the Setup program also delete the databases and devices. The deletion of the SMS site will not affect packages previously sent to distribution points or installed on clients.

Installing New SMS Components

During the installation of the primary site server, you had the option to copy binaries required for SMS site systems running on different hardware platforms than the site server's. By running Setup from the SMS CD, you can install the necessary binaries after the initial installation to accommodate the addition of other system types. In this way, you can also add and remove any of the optional SMS components listed earlier.

Installing a Secondary Site Server

The following sections will consider areas surrounding the installation, configuration, and modification of a secondary site server. But first, let's review some of the basic characteristics of a secondary site:

- Secondary sites do not require a SQL Server database.

- Secondary sites cannot be directly administered and generally do not have a dedicated administrator.

- Secondary sites are always child sites.

- Secondary sites cannot be parent sites.

The installation of a secondary site cannot begin until after the primary site it will be a child of has been installed. The installation of the secondary site can then be initiated in one of two ways, as detailed in the next sections.

Performing the Installation from the CD-ROM

SMS 2 allows you to initiate the setup of a secondary site from the computer that will be the secondary site server. This option is the best to choose when a qualified installer will be physically present at the secondary site during installation. The basic installation steps are as follows:

1. Initiate SMS Setup from the secondary site server's CD-ROM.

2. Select the option to install a secondary site.

3. Enter registration information and CD-KEY.

4. Enter the secondary site's unique site code.

5. Enter the secondary site's SMS Service Account information.

6. Select site system platforms.

7. Select optional components and installation directory.

8. Enter the parent site's site code, server name, and then select the initial connection type.

9. Enter the connection account information to use when attaching to the parent site's SMS_SITE share.

10. Confirm settings and finish.

11. Create an address from the parent site back to the secondary site. This is necessary for the parent site to communicate with the child site.

Performing a Network Installation by Using Files from the Network or the CD-ROM

When a qualified installer will not be physically present at the secondary site, it is possible to initiate the installation from the primary site that will be the secondary site's parent. The Secondary Site Installation Wizard can transfer files via a sender to the secondary site, or, if a copy of the SMS Setup file is available at the secondary site, the Setup program can be directed to locate them on a drive at the secondary site server.

Approximately 59MB of data are transferred from the parent site to the secondary site if local source files are not used.

The Secondary Site Installation Wizard requires you to provide information similar to that needed when the setup is initiated locally at the secondary site server. The wizard can, however, take care of creating the address from the parent site to the secondary site automatically.

Configuring Site System Roles

Many of the duties performed within an SMS site are modular and can be distributed among a number of site systems. The specific duty performed identifies the role that a given site system plays.

The following sections detail the assignment of various site system roles, including component server, logon point, distribution point, client access point, and software metering server.

Configuring Component Servers

A component server is usually used to lessen the load on the site server, provide redundancy, or perform a function not supported by the site server. The primary use of a component server is as a sender, especially in the case of a remote access service (RAS) sender.

Only NT 4–based systems with SP4 and later can be component servers.

Configuring Logon Points

Logon points are the locations from which clients can execute a logon script to initiate installation.

Assigning the logon point role is directly linked to the types of discovery you enable and their configuration, as follows:

Enabling Windows Networking Logon Discovery (see Figure 2.2) assigns the logon point role to all NT domain controllers that are members of the listed domains.

FIGURE 2.2

Windows Networking Logon Discovery logon points are assigned by domain.

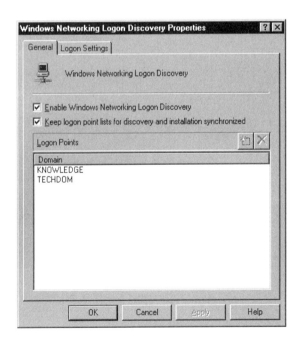

Enabling NetWare Bindery Logon Discovery enables the discovery of NetWare 3.*x* clients. Enter as logon points the names of the bindery-based servers to designate as logon points.

Enabling NetWare NDS Logon Discovery enables the discovery of NetWare 4.*x* clients. Enter as logon points the names of the volumes in the NDS tree to designate as logon points.

After establishing logon points for discovery, you will still need to populate the logon points with logon scripts to be read by the clients if you want them to install client software. To simplify this process and to ensure that the logon point list remains valid, you can specify to synchronize the logon points for discovery and installation.

Only NT 4–based systems and later, with SP3, SP4, and later, and NetWare 3.*x* Bindery and 4.*x* NDS can be logon points.

Configuring Distribution Points

Distribution points (see Figure 2.3) are used to hold packages to be installed on clients. The role of a distribution point can be assigned to NT servers, NT shares, and NetWare volumes.

You can reduce the workload on the site server by not using it as a distribution point.

At least one distribution point must be available to each client type.

Distribution points can be logically grouped, to simplify their selection during package disbursement. For example, you may wish to create a distribution point group that includes selected NT-based and NetWare-based distribution points to simplify distribution of packages to collections with mixed membership.

Systems with NT 3.51, NT 4, NT 4 with SP3, NT 4 with SP4 or later, NT 4 Enterprise with SP4 or later, NT 5, NetWare 3.*x* Bindery, and NetWare 4.*x* NDS can be distribution points.

Configuring Client Access Points

Client access points (see Figure 2.4) are places where clients can learn of new advertisements and configuration changes. Client access points are used also to report hardware and software inventory.

FIGURE 2.4

Assigning the role of a client access point

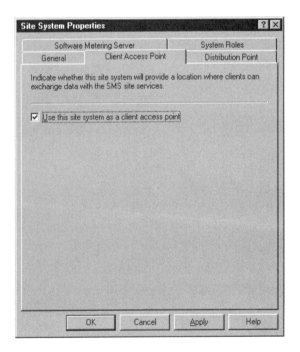

The role of a client access point can be assigned to NT servers, NT shares, and NetWare volumes.

At least one client access point must exist for each client type.

Systems with NT 4 with SP3, NT 4 with SP4 or later, NT 4 Enterprise with SP4 or later, NT 5, NetWare 3.*x* Bindery, and NetWare 4.*x* NDS can be client access points.

Configuring Software Metering Servers

Software metering servers (see Figure 2.5) act as intermediaries between client-side agents and the site server managing the software metering database.

FIGURE 2.5

Configuring a software metering server

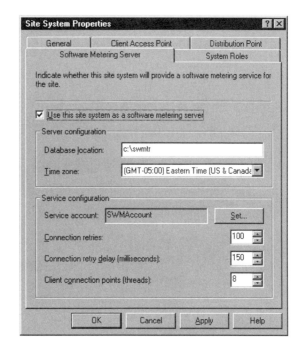

Clients report software usage to the software metering server, which passes the information to the site server at scheduled intervals.

Systems with NT 4 with SP4 or later, NT 4 Enterprise with SP4 or later, and NT 5 can be software metering servers.

Configuring the SMS Administrator Console

Although the SMS Administrator Console is not a true site system role, it is a modular component of SMS. The SMS Administrator Console is your interface for the SMS database.

The SMS Administrator Console can be run on any Windows NT 4 system with SP4 or later and Internet Explorer 4.01 with SP1 installed.

The Console can be configured to support only the required SMS features.

Configuring an SMS Site Hierarchy

Unit 1 includes much useful information on the relationships between systems and sites in an SMS hierarchy. This section on configuration provides an overview of how those relationships are implemented.

Configuring Site Addresses

If you think of senders as the roadways between sites, then addresses would be synonymous with the maps. Site addresses define which sender to use when transferring data to another site, the schedule of time during which a sender can be used, and the amount of bandwidth consumption allowed.

Multiple addresses and senders to a single site can be established to provide redundancy or greater data capacity. When configuring a site address, you must enter or confirm the settings using the General, Schedule, and Rate Limits tabs:

General

Destination site code   The name of the site to which the address will direct data.

Relative address priority   A priority number used to determine which address should be used first when multiple addresses are available. The lowest priority number receives precedence and two addresses to the same sender cannot have the same priority.

New addresses to the same sender receive by default a lower priority than preexisting addresses to the same sender.

Site server name   The name of the site server at the destination site.

Account   An account that is valid at the destination site server.

Schedule

Availability   The time periods that jobs can be passed via the address. You can specify the minimum priority that a job must have to be passed during a given period. For example, in Figure 2.6 traffic is resricted based on priority of jobs during the day..

FIGURE 2.6

Configuring address availability for specific periods of time

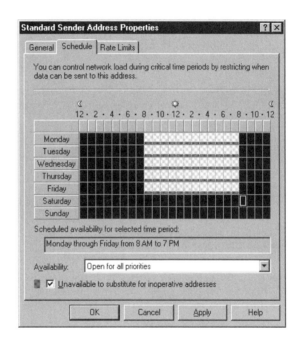

Unavailable to substitute for inoperative addresses   Select this option to prevent this address from being used during specific times as an alternate route.

Rate Limits

Setting rate limits can help prevent SMS from monopolizing bandwidth between sites. By default, SMS's bandwidth consumption is not restricted; however, you can limit the transfer rates to a percentage of the potential bandwidth during specific hours of the day.

Adding and Configuring Senders, Consisting of Standard, Courier, and RAS

Senders are responsible for coordinating the data flow between sites. The following list details each sender and its requirements:

Standard sender   When a reliable LAN or WAN link with available bandwidth exists between sites, it is generally preferable to connect the sites using the standard sender. This is the simplest of the senders to configure, as it works in conjunction with the existing network protocols.

Neither the standard sender nor the courier sender requires configuration by the administrator.

Asynchronous RAS sender   This sender can be used to establish site connections over standard dial-up lines. This sender requires that Microsoft RAS be running on the server that will host the RAS sender. The information about the dial-up account to be used is specified when the address for the sender is created.

SNA RAS sender   This sender is used to establish and maintain a logical unit pair connection between sites installed with Microsoft SNS Server. Two modes of configuration, batch and interactive, are supported for the connection.

ISDN RAS sender   This sender establishes a RAS connection over an ISDN line.

X.25 RAS sender   This sender establishes a RAS connection over an X.25 network.

Courier sender   This sender is used when network connectivity cannot be established between sites or when the amount of data that must be sent is too prohibitive. The courier sender is installed automatically and cannot be configured or deleted. To use the courier sender, however, you must still create an address for the destination site. The creation and receipt of parcels is controlled manually through the Courier Sender Manager, shown in Figure 2.7.

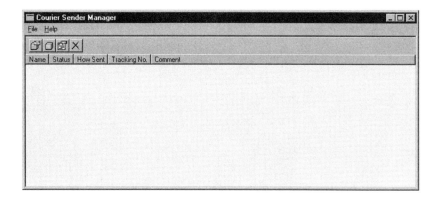

The decision to use one sender over another is usually a matter of cost versus convenience. When the network can support the direct connection of sites over the LAN or WAN, the standard sender should be used. If the network is already saturated or if the connection is unstable, then you should consider one of the various RAS senders. The use of the courier sender should be reserved for sites without connectivity or for times when the configured senders cannot support a large periodic transfer.

If multiple connectors will be required, it is possible to assign them to various site systems, which are then called component servers. Each site system can support multiple senders, but only one sender of each type can be installed per site system.

Implementing Parent-Child Relationships

The relationship between parent and child sites defines the SMS site hierarchy. Designing an SMS site hierarchy was covered in depth in Unit 1, Planning. In this section, the focus is on how to implement your SMS site hierarchy.

Remember that primary sites can be parent sites, child sites, or both. Secondary sites can only be child sites.

When a secondary site is created, it automatically becomes a child site of the primary site specified during installation. By viewing the properties of the child site, as seen in Figure 2.8, you can identify the relationship between a child site and its parent site.

FIGURE 2.8

The properties page of
a child site

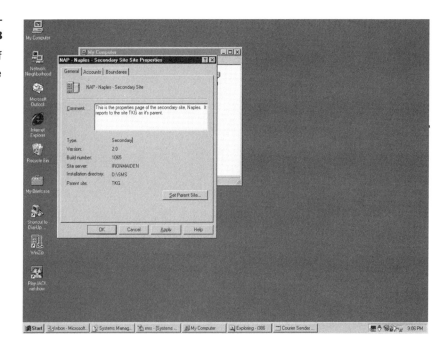

For primary sites, you can specify the site that a primary child site is linked to by configuring the Set Parent Site option.

The assignment of a site as a child site is always done from the site that will become the child site, not from the parent site.

Primary sites are initially configured as stand-alone sites. The relationships among primary sites must be configured manually.

Removing a Site from the Hierarchy

You may choose to remove a site from the hierarchy to have it act as a stand-alone site (primary sites only) or to reposition it in the hierarchy. You can change the parent of a secondary site only by reinstalling.

Specifying a new parent site for a primary site or removing it from the hierarchy is performed from the Set Parent Site window. To remove a site from the hierarchy, configure it to be a central site.

Installing, Configuring, and Modifying a Primary Site Server

1. True/False: Any ODBC-compliant database can be used as the location for the SMS database.

2. True/False: Microsoft SQL Server must be installed on the primary site server.

3. Version _____ with SP 5 and Version _____ of Microsoft SQL Server can be used as the SMS database server.

4. SQL 6.5 with SP 5 is installed automatically when an _____ setup is performed.

5. True/False: If Microsoft SQL Server is already installed on the target computer, only a custom setup can be performed.

6. Separate SQL devices must exist for the SMS _____ and _____ segments.

7. True/False: The SMS database cannot be assigned to a preexisting SQL device.

8. The default names of the SMS database devices are _____ and _____.

9. When using SQL 7, device names are not required.

10. SQL devices can be expanded by using the DISK RESIZE statement or SQL Server _____ Manager.

11. Both SQL Enterprise Manager and the _____ DATABASE statement can be used to expand SQL databases.

12. What are the three security modes that Microsoft SQL Server supports?

13. True/False: When using integrated security, the SQL Server must be located in the same domain as the primary site server.

14. To improve the speed of queries, you can increase the size of the _____ database.

15. The required minimum lock setting is _____.

16. All SMS site servers and administrative systems require that Internet Explorer version _____ be installed.

17. SMS site servers can be installed on computers with either Intel Pentium or _____ processors.

18. The site server requires a minimum of _____MB of free space.

19. True /False: The express version of the SMS Setup program automatically assigns a unique site code.

20. The site code is limited to _____ characters.

21. True/False: The site domain is the name of the domain of which the SQL Server is a member.

22. The _____ account is used by SMS site systems to communicate with each other.

23. True/False: By default, the custom setup only installs the SMS server and the SMS Administrator Console.

24. The drive selected to hold the SMS components must be formatted with the _____ file system.

25. Each SMS Administrator Console requires _____ SQL Server connections to be configured.

Installing a Secondary Site Server

26. Installation of a secondary site can be initiated from the _____ or by running the _____ from the primary site.

27. True/False: A primary site must be installed before installing any secondary sites.

28. True/False: A secondary site server must be configured as a domain member.

29. True/False: Support for the software metering service is installed automatically on secondary site servers.

30. The _____ sender allows the installation of secondary sites across a dial-up line.

31. True/False: The SMS administrator must create an address for the secondary site manually at its parent site.

32. The connection account used to connect to the parent site must have full rights to the _____ share.

33. True/False: Secondary sites are always child sites.

Configuring Site System Roles

34. Only _____–based computers can be site systems.

35. The primary use of a _____ server is as a RAS sender.

36. True/False: A single site system can perform multiple SMS roles.

37. The role of a logon point can be assigned to domain controllers and to NetWare _____–based, and NetWare _____–based systems.

38. Windows Networking Logon Discovery points are assigned by _____.

39. _____ points are used to hold packages to be installed on clients.

STUDY QUESTIONS

40. True/False: The site server must always perform the role of a distribution point.

41. True/False: Distribution points can be logically grouped to simplify package disbursement.

42. Clients receive notification of new advertisements from _____ points.

43. Clients report hardware and software inventory changes to _____ points.

44. The role of a client access point can be assigned to _____,
_____, and NetWare _____.

45. The SMS administrator can run on any _____ system with SP
_____ or later.

Configuring an SMS Site Hierarchy

46. Site _____ define which sender to use when transferring data to another site.

47. True/False: Multiple addresses can be configured to a single site.

48. True/False: A single sender can be configured with varying degrees of permitted bandwidth use for different times of the day.

49. When multiple addresses are configured for the same sender, the one with the
_____ precedence number is chosen.

50. True/False: The latest address created to a given sender always has the highest precedence level granted by default.

51. The _____ sender is used across a LAN or a WAN.

52. The four types of RAS senders are _____, _____, _____, and _____.

53. The _____ sender is used between sites without physical connectivity.

54. The maximum number of parent sites a primary or secondary site can have is _____.

55. Only _____ sites can be stand-alone sites.

56. Removing a site from the hierarchy is done from the _____ window.

57. When moving the SMS database to a new SQL Server you should use _____ to move the database before reconfiguring the site.

58. True/False: All site systems within a site must be installed on the same hardware platform.

SAMPLE TEST

2-1   Which of the following versions of SQL Server can play the role of an SMS database server?

    A. Microsoft SQL Server 1.0

    B. Microsoft SQL Server 4.2

    C. Microsoft SQL Server 6.5

    D. Microsoft SQL Server 6.5 with SP 5

    E. Microsoft SQL Server 7

    F. Any ODBC-compliant database server

2-2   The administrator of Example Company is planning to install SMS 2 at its headquarters. The administrator has been given the following objectives to meet:

Required result: Install all mandatory and optional SMS components on the primary site server.

Desired result: Create the SMS database on the corporation's preexisting Microsoft SQL 7 server.

Solution: The administrator recommends using the SQL Server as the primary site server and performing an express setup.

Which of the following statements best describes the effectiveness of the administrator's plan?

    A. The solution meets both the required and the desired objectives.

    B. The solution meets only the required objective.

    C. The solution meets only the desired objective.

    D. The solution meets neither the required nor the desired objective.

SAMPLE TEST

2-3   The administrator of Example Company has hired an SMS consultant to install SMS at their site. The consultant has been given the following objective:

Required result: Install a primary site with all components, utilizing the company's existing Microsoft SQL Server.

Solution: The consultant recommends creating the SMS databases using space available on the accounting departments SQL devices. After the databases are created, the consultant recommends doing a custom installation and selecting all components.

Which of the following statements best describes the effectiveness of the consultant's plan?

    A. The plan meets the objective and is the best possible solution.

    B. The plan meets the objective and is a good solution.

    C. The plan meets the objective but is not a desirable solution.

    D. The plan does not meet the objectives.

2-4   When installing both the SMS database and SMS metering database, how many SQL devices are required?

    A. One

    B. Two

    C. Three

    D. Four

2-5   Which of the following statements are true when the primary site server and SQL Server are not members of the same domain?

    A. Integrated security can be used.

    B. Standard security can be used.

C. The SQL Server's domain must trust the primary site server's domain.

D. The primary site server's domain must trust the SQL Server's domain.

E. None of the above.

2-6   After expanding the site boundaries to include several additional subnets, Example Company's administrator has noticed that queries performed through the SMS Administrator Console are responding quite slowly.

Which of the following steps should the SQL administrator perform?

A. Increase the size of tempdb.

B. Increase the number of concurrent connections allowed.

C. Increase the number of open locks.

D. Increase the number of open database objects.

2-7   Which of the following statements about SMS site codes are correct?

A. Secondary sites inherit the same site code as their parent site.

B. Site codes must contain three characters.

C. Site code uniqueness is confirmed during installation.

D. All sites in the SMS hierarchy must have unique site codes.

2-8   Which of the following information must be provided during the installation of a secondary site?

A. The SMS site code to be used at the secondary site.

B. The name of the domain where the secondary site is being installed.

C. The name of the domain where the primary site is installed.

D. The SMS site code in use at the parent site.

2-9 Which of the following steps can you perform to change the site code in use at an SMS site?

    A. Reinstall the site.

    B. Use SQL Enterprise Manager.

    C. Use the `codegen.exe` program.

    D. Use the SQL Administrator Console.

2-10 Example Company will have 10 administrators requiring a total of five different levels of permissions within the SMS site hierarchy. A separate division manages the SQL Server. How many SQL accounts will be required to support the 10 administrators.

    A. A single account is sufficient (1 account).

    B. A single account for each privilege level is required (5 accounts).

    C. A unique account is required for each administrator (10 accounts).

    D. Each administrator will require two accounts (20 accounts).

2-11 After installing a secondary site (NAP) below the primary site (TKG), the administrator finds that she is not able to distribute packages to the secondary site. Which of the following steps must the administrator perform?

    A. Create a new address at the primary site that points to the secondary site.

    B. Create a new address at the secondary site that points to the parent site.

    C. Create a new sender at the primary site that can communicate with the secondary site.

    D. Create a new sender at the secondary site that can communicate with the primary site.

    E. Reinstall the secondary site.

2-12 What must Example Company's administrator do in order to use Novell NetWare 4.11 servers as logon points?

    A. Install NetWare Bindery Support.

    B. Install NetWare NDS Support.

    C. Install the SMS Administrator Console NLM on the server.

    D. Novell NetWare 4.11 servers cannot be used as logon points.

2-13 Example Company's administrator wants to limit the amount of bandwidth consumed between SMS sites during the hours of 8:00 A.M. and 5:00 P.M. Additionally, only medium priority jobs and above should be allowed to pass during the restricted times. Which of the following steps must the administrator perform?

    A. Configure the permitted job priority from the availability page of the sender's schedule page.

    B. Configure the permitted job priority from the availability section of the address's schedule page.

    C. Configure the permitted bandwidth consumption from the sender's rate limits page.

    D. Configure the permitted bandwidth consumption from the address's rate limits page.

2-14 The Example Company is planning to move the SMS database to a new Microsoft SQL Server. Which of the following statements about the SQL Server is true?

    A. The SQL Server must run Microsoft SQL Server 6.5 with SP 5 or Microsoft SQL Server 7.

    B. The SQL Server must reside on an Intel Pentium computer.

    C. The SMS provider must be installed on the SQL Server.

    D. The SMS Setup program can be used to physically move the database to the new server.

2-15 Example Company's administrator wants to reduce the workload on the primary site server. Which of the following steps should she perform?

    A. Relocate distribution points from the site server to other systems.

    B. Move the SMS provider to the SQL Server.

    C. Reassign child sites to other parent sites.

    D. Reduce the number of subnets in the site boundaries.

U N I T

3

Configuring and
Managing Resources

Test Objectives

- **Configure software and hardware inventory collection for a site.**
  - Enable and configure hardware inventory collection.
  - Enable and configure software inventory files to be scanned and collected.

- **Manage inventory data.**
  - View inventory data, including history.
  - Use the SMS Administrator Console to manage inventory data.
  - Customize inventory data.

- **Distribute software.**
  - Use SMS Installer to produce installation executable files.
  - Create a query to locate target computers.
  - Create a collection of target computers.
  - Create a package, program, and advertisement to distribute software.
  - Monitor the software distribution process by using status messages.
  - Use the SMS client software to run or install a program on a client computer.
  - Remove advertised software from distribution points.

- **Configure and use software metering.**
  - Configure software metering servers and client components.
  - Add products to be licensed.
  - Configure licensing options.
  - Exclude products from being metered.
  - Meter software.
  - Manage software metering data.
  - Generate reports and graphs.

Exam objectives are subject to change at any time without prior notice and at Microsoft's sole discretion. Please visit Microsoft's Training and Certification Web site (www.microsoft.com/Train_Cert/) for the most current listing of exam objectives.

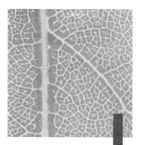

In this unit, we'll review the procedures for collecting and reporting hardware and software inventory data. Additionally, we'll consider the methods used to distribute software and to provide metering and licensing capabilities.

Configuring Software and Hardware Inventory Collection for a Site

For many administrators, the primary use of SMS is to provide an accurate account of hardware and software throughout an organization.

Being able to properly determine that computer systems meet certain criteria is essential to numerous functions, including the proper distribution of software.

Computer systems must be discovered before they can become available for hardware or software inventory collection.

However, determining system resources requires more than simply discovering the existence and location of computer systems. The following sections review the specifics of hardware and software inventory collection.

Enabling and Configuring Hardware Inventory Collection

Because inventory requirements at different sites usually vary, hardware inventory is configured on a per site basis. The configuration is controlled by the settings of each site's hardware inventory agent properties.

Hardware Inventory Agent

By modifying the properties of the hardware inventory agent (see Figure 3.1) you can selectively enable or disable hardware inventory and specify the frequency with which the inventory should be updated.

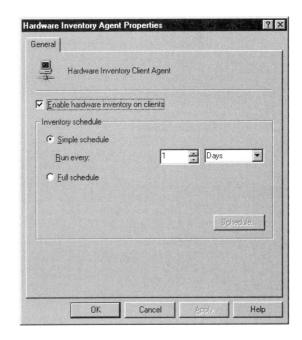

When you choose the option to enable hardware inventory on client computers, the hardware inventory agent will be installed on all 32-bit and 16-bit clients discovered within the site.

In addition to enabling hardware inventory, you must specify the schedule for clients to collect and report inventory to a client access point (CAP). You can use either the simple schedule or the full schedule to specify when inventory should be taken.

Simple Schedule   The simple schedule allows you to specify the number of hours, days, or weeks that should be used as a recurring interval for inventory.

Full Schedule   The full schedule allows greater flexibility than the simple schedule. Using the full schedule you can specify a start time, following which the system will implement inventory collection based on intervals of minutes, hours, days, weeks, or months. You can also specify that inventory should be collected on a specific day of the week or month.

Hardware Inventory Collection Process

Once you have enabled the hardware inventory process for 32-bit clients of a site, the following steps are involved in the reporting process:

This section deals only with the portions of the inventory process for which the client system is responsible.

1. Client component installation manager (CCIM) (Ccim32.dll) installs hardware inventory components on the client.

2. CCIM creates the %Windir%\MS\SMS\Clicomp\Hinv directory.

3. CCIM directs Mofcomp.exe to compile SMS_def.mof into the CCIM object manager to set the hardware inventory defaults.

SMS_def.mof is the default management object format (MOF) file used to determine which hardware properties should be included in the inventory. SMS_def.mof can be altered to modify the properties reported, using any text editor or using the MOF manager (graphic tool).

4. Clisvcl.exe determines the scheduled interval for inventory to be updated.

5. Hinv32.exe is run at the scheduled interval to collect and store inventory.

The first time inventory is enabled, it will perform a full hardware inventory of the system after a 15-minute delay.

6. Hinv32.exe bases the information it will report on the CIMOM schema and any NOIDMIFs and IDMIFs that are implemented.

MIF files are used to augment the inventory collection requirements for specific clients or sites. NOIDMIFs increase the number of parameters reported for individual systems, whereas IDMIFs provide the site hierarchy with additional classes and architectures. The entries included in the NOID-MIFs are merged into the CIMOM schema for individual clients.

7. `Hinv32.exe` generates either a `Hinvdat.hic` or a `Hinvdata.hid` file, depending on whether the inventory collected is the complete inventory (.hic) or just the inventory changes, or delta (.hid).

A complete hardware inventory file (`Hinvdat.hic`) is generated only when inventory is first run, unless a `Hinvdata.hid` file is passed that does not correspond to an entry, sites are changed, or the recorded inventory is corrupt. The process of forcing a complete hardware inventory file by the system is called *resynchronization*.

8. `Hinv32.exe` copies the inventory file (i.e., `Hinvdat.hic`) with an `.inv` extension to the client's `%Windir%\MS\SMS\Clicomp\Hinv\Outbox` directory.

9. `Hinv32.exe` renames any IDMIF files it locates in the `%Windir%\MS\SMS\Idmifs` directory with an `.inv` extension.

10. The copy queue manager (`Cqmgr32.dll`) copies all `.inv` files to the client access point's `Inventry.box` directory with an `.nmh` extension.

Enabling and Configuring Software Inventory Files to be Scanned and Collected

The software inventory collection process can be used both to identify which software is installed on systems and to collect copies of specific files.

The enabling and scheduling of the software inventory collection agent is identical to that of the hardware inventory collection agent described earlier in this unit.

Software Inventory Agent

The software inventory agent is configured on a per site basis. The properties page of the software inventory agent consists of three tabs: General, Inventory Collection, and File Collection.

General   The General tab is used to enable the software inventory agent on clients within the site, and to specify the frequency of software inventory collection.

When deciding which aspects of inventory collection to use, if any, you should take into consideration client-side requirements and network bandwidth limitations. Clients to be inventoried require a minimum of 3MB available virtual memory, plus at least 2MB of free disk space; the collection of files will substantially increase the hard disk space requirements.

Inventory Collection   The Inventory Collection tab (see Figure 3.2) is used to specify the types of files that you want to inventory and how they should be categorized.

F I G U R E 3.2

Configuring inventory collection settings

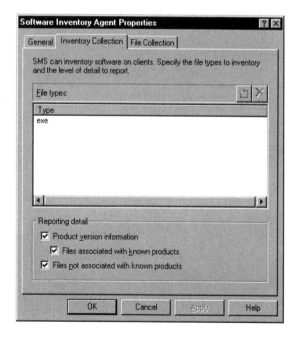

The types of files you want to inventory are determined by the file extensions you assign. By default, only files ending in .exe will be inventoried.

Wildcards are valid in identifying files to inventory; however, you cannot use *.*.

Inventoried files containing file details can be listed by manufacturer. You can also group together files known to be associated with specific applications.

File Collection   The File Collection tab (see Figure 3.3) is used to enable copying of specified file from SMS clients. To prevent placing an unnecessary burden on the site server, you can limit the amount of megabytes that can be collected by clients per session.

FIGURE 3.3

A copy of config.sys can be collected from clients.

Collected files are deleted automatically after they have aged 90 days. To limit the amount of space required to store collected files, no more than five copies of each file are collected within any given 90-day period.

Because file collection is performed by first making a copy of the files to be copied to the server on the client, significant disk space overhead can be associated with this procedure, on the client, the CAP, and the site server. As a general rule, you should make sure that 10 percent of the client's disk space is available.

In order to limit the amount of space used, you can specify the combined maximum size of files that can be collected per client. If you do restrict this, remember that individual files exceeding the size limit on certain clients will not be collected.

Managing Inventory Data

To manage inventory for a site effectively, you'll need to understand how to view both current and historical inventory data, using the SMS Administrator Console. Also, you might need to extend the inventory functions for a given site or client. This section will discuss how you can best manage and customize the inventory collection process.

Viewing Inventory Data, Including History

The Resource Explorer (see Figure 3.4) is used to view inventory data collected from within the site on a per client basis in each inventory category, including hardware, software, and history. Simply select the client whose inventory you wish to evaluate from within a collection, click on Task, and select Resource Explorer.

Historical hardware inventory can be viewed from the Hardware History folder using Resource Explorer. How long historical data are available depends on the database maintenance task Delete Aged History. By default, historical data are stored for 90 days.

F I G U R E   3.4

Viewing the inventory
of IRONMASTER,
using the Resource
Explorer

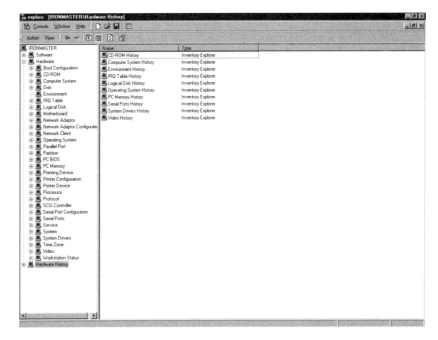

Using the SMS Administrator Console to Manage Inventory Data

Some questions may require you to know the location to access within the SMS Administrator Console to configure certain settings.

Remember that the administrative program is a snap-in to the Microsoft Management Console (MMC) and can be customized. For example, you can create a version of the MMC that displays only certain portions of the SMS hierarchy (e.g., packages, collections). To create a custom MMC, click on Start, click on Run, type **MMC**, and hit Enter; then add or remove your snap-ins, configure the console the way you want it to look, and save what you've done.

Customizing Inventory Data

Inventory collection can be enhanced for specific sites and clients by modifying the SMS_def.mof and by using IDMIFs and NOIDMIFs.

The initial inventory schema is loaded into CIMOM from the SMS_def.mof file. You need to take special care when making adjustments to SMS_def.mof because improper configuration can unnecessarily burden the inventory process. Although Microsoft has designed the SMS_def.mof file to support all required properties for Desktop Management Task Force (DMTF) compliance, most of the properties are disabled by default to reduce inventory requirements.

IDMIFs can extend the hardware inventory that is collected within a given site, as well as increasing the architectures (i.e., PC) and property classes (i.e., Memory) available within a site.

Remember that IDMIFs and NOIDMIFs, in addition to an SMS_def.mof file, are used to increase inventory capabilities.

NOIDMIFs can increase the hardware inventory classes reported on for specific clients. Remember that NOIDMIFs extend the property classes for individual systems, not groups of systems or sites.

Distributing Software

Software distribution is generally considered one of the key reasons for implementing SMS in an organization. Because of its importance, you'll probably be asked several questions on all phases of software distribution.

Using SMS Installer to Produce Installation Executable Files

Using the SMS Installer is the preferred way to create installation scripts. The SMS Installer must be installed first on a site server, and then on a computer whose hardware and software configuration matches that of the systems to which you will be deploying the software. The computer used as the baseline is called the *reference server* and the computer systems you will deploy to are called *target computers*.

After installing the SMS Installer on the reference computer, you can create complete packages and package definition files using the Installation Expert. Each package created will be a single executable program file containing all of the required source files and necessary supporting files.

Creating a Query to Locate Target Computers

Although the advertisement of packages is ultimately done to collections, it is often a good policy to first validate potential collection members by generating a query. If the query results return the desired results, it is possible to then build a collection based on the query.

Remember that although a collection can be based on a query, the query logic stored with a collection is independent of the query itself. If a query on which a collection is based is later modified, the modifications affect only the query itself; the changes are not applied to the collection's selection criteria.

Creating a Collection to Locate Target Computers

Collection membership can be based either on direct membership rules or on a query. When a client is entered as a member of a collection using direct membership, its collection membership is not contingent on meeting the criteria of the query. When using a query to define collection membership, the logic of the query is saved with the collection. This makes the collection independent of the original query, which can then be modified or deleted without affecting the rules defining collection membership.

When creating a collection based on a query, it is a good practice to schedule the collection to be updated on a periodic basis. Membership in the collection can be granted or revoked to SMS clients when the collection is updated.

Creating a Package, Program, and Advertisement to Distribute Software

The process of software distribution uses three basic objects: packages, programs, and advertisements.

Packages

Creating a package is the first stage in software distribution. Packages are used to define the properties of the application to be distributed. They can be created manually or by importing a package definition file using the Create Package from Definition Wizard.

You should become familiar with the purpose served by each of the package definition property tabs Each of the configurable settings you'll encounter when manually creating a package is summarized briefly in the following sections.

General The General tab defines the basic package properties, including Name, Version, Publisher, Language, Comments, and the icon to be displayed for the application. Of these, the only required entry is the Name field, which defines the name of package. Package names can be between 1 and 50 characters, and must be unique within a site.

Data Source The Data Source tab (see Figure 3.5) defines the location of the application's source files. This information is used when the system copies the source files from the data source to the distribution points.

FIGURE 3.5

Defining the package
data source properties

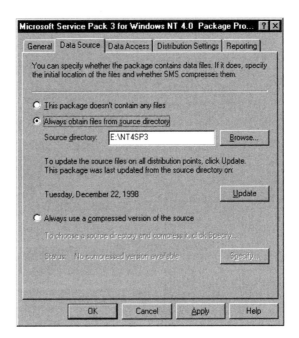

The three distinct options that you can specify are explained here:

This package doesn't contain any files This option (selected by default) is used when the application defined by the package is already installed on the clients. This allows you to force the client to run an application that is already installed.

Always obtain files from source directory This option is used to specify the location of the application's source files. If the source files have changed since originally distributed, you can force an update to all distribution points by clicking on the Update button.

Always use a compressed version of the source This option is used when the source media may not be available at a later time. A copy of the specified source is compressed on the site server, to be used as the distribution source later.

Data Access The Data Access tab (see Figure 3.6) specifies whether to use the default share name or a specific share name on distribution servers. This tab also defines how to handle connected users during package updates.

F I G U R E 3.6

Defining data access properties

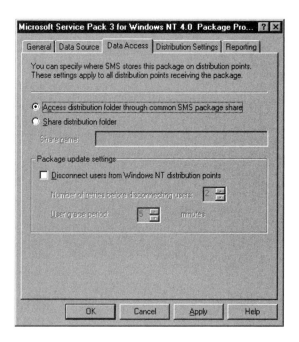

Access distribution folder through common SMS package share This default option is used to accept the standard SMS package share (i.e., SMSPKGD) as the location to store the package on distribution points.

Share distribution folder This option allows you to specify a unique share name and subdirectory to be used by the application on distribution points.

Package update settings This option can be configured to forcibly disconnect users from distribution points during updates. You can configure the number of attempts the system should make to update the files before disconnecting users and the grace period of time, if any, to allow users to remain connected once the option to disconnect has been chosen.

Distribution Settings   The Distribution Settings tab (see Figure 3.7) is used to define the sending priority, preferred sender, and update schedule.

F I G U R E 3.7

Configuring distribu-
tion settings

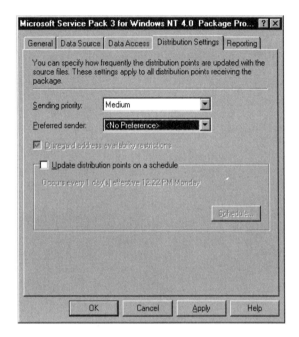

Sending priority   This setting defines the priority (low, medium, or high) that the package should receive when being transferred to child sites. The default priority is medium.

Preferred sender   This setting allows you to enter a preference, if any, of the sender type to use when transferring the package to child sites.

Disregard address availability restrictions   This setting overrides address restrictions in order to allow this specific package to be transmitted to child sites, even when the address specifies the sender as closed. This option is available only if you specify a preferred sender.

Update distribution points on a schedule   This option can be used to update distribution points, based on a defined schedule. By default, this option is not enabled.

Reporting The Reporting tab provides the option of specifying a MIF file name, Name, Version, and Publisher to be used by the system in associating inventory MIF files on the client. The default option is simply to use the properties defined in the General settings tab.

Programs

Programs are the set of commands that will be executed by the clients assigned to a given package. For example, the package definition file for Microsoft Office 97 defines programs for Custom, Manual, and Typical installations, in addition to Uninstall.

Programs are defined automatically when you use a package definition file; otherwise they must be manually created. The following sections detail the tabs you will encounter when setting up a program manually.

General The General tab (see Figure 3.8) allows you to define the basic properties of the program, including the following:

FIGURE 3.8

Defining program
properties

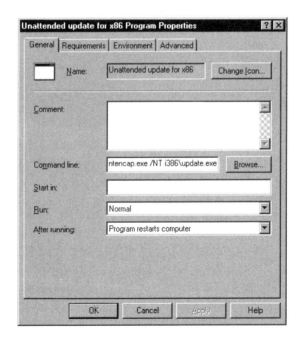

Name This required entry provides the name of the program displayed to clients to whom it is advertised.

Comment   The optional comment can be used to provide clients with a more detailed description of the program.

Command line   This is the command sequence to be executed by the client (e.g., Setup /min).

Start in   This specifies the directory where the command line executable can be located.

Run   This setting controls whether the program will run in a normal screen (default), minimized, maximized, or hidden.

After running   The setting specifying the action required at completion of the program. Options include No action, SMS restarts computer, Program restarts computer, and SMS logs user off.

Requirements   The Requirements tab (see Figure 3.9) provides system requirements used to determine the targeted clients' capacity for running a given program. The requirements you can specify are described here.

FIGURE 3.9

Specifying program
requirements

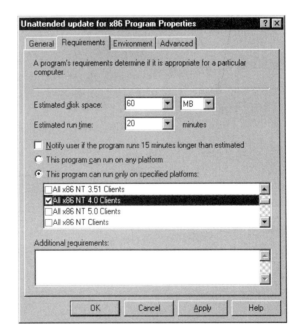

Estimated disk space   The amount of space in KB, MB, or GB required to run the program on the client. An entry of Unknown can be specified.

Estimated run time   The amount of time the program will require to run on the client. An entry of Unknown can be specified.

Notify user if the program runs 15 minutes longer than estimated   This option can be used to notify the user only when an estimated run time is provided.

This program can run on any platform   This option allows advertisements of the program to be made to clients regardless of platform.

This program can run only on specified platforms   This option should be used when members of a heterogeneous collection are not all capable of running a program because of hardware differences. This option is commonly used with service packs.

Additional requirements   This option is used to provide a comment to users. Steps the user should take before or after installation should be noted here.

Environment   The Environment tab (see Figure 3.10) is used to define all of the necessary environmental factors required for the program to run properly.

F I G U R E   3.10

Configuring the environmental requirements

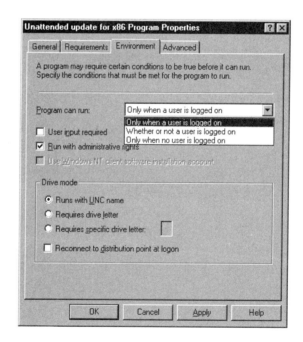

The environmental factors that can be specified are listed here:

Program can run   Used to configure the program's ability to run with or without a locally logged-on user account. The default option of running programs Only When a User Is Logged On must be used unless the client is running Microsoft Windows NT. Choosing the option to run the program Only When No User Is Logged On causes the program to be run in the security context of the administrative account after the user logs off. The option to run the program Whether Or Not a User Is Logged On uses the Local System account.

User input required   Used when the program is not automated and requires user interaction. You must select the option Only When a User Is Logged On to enable this option.

Run with administrative rights   Used in conjunction with the option Only When a User Is Logged On, to specify that the current user must have administrative rights to run the program.

Use Windows NT client software installation account   Selected when you want to use the Windows NT client software installation account defined in the Software Distribution component configuration settings. This option is not available when Only When a User Is Logged On is specified.

Drive mode   Used to specify the type of connection supported by the program to the distribution point: Runs with UNC (default), Requires Drive Letter, or Requires Specific Drive Letter.

Reconnect to distribution point at logon   Used to reconnect the drive to the distribution point automatically following a logon sequence.

Advanced   The Advanced tab (see Figure 3.11) is used to define supporting steps that must be taken to ensure that the program is properly installed, removed, or disabled.

Run another program first   Specifies a separate package or program that must be run in advance.

When program is assigned   Specifies that a program should run only once, regardless of the user who logs on, or once for every user who logs on. As this option is logon name dependent, it can only be used in conjunction with the Only When a User Is Logged On option.

Remove software when it is no longer advertised   Removes program-related network application shortcuts from clients.

Disable this program on computers where it is advertised   Disables the program on clients by recanting the advertisements.

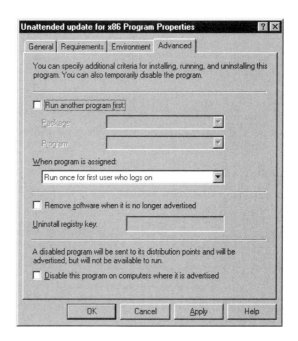

Advertisements

After defining both the package and the program, you must next create an advertisement to make clients aware of the package's existence at the distribution points. The creation of a new advertisement requires only the configuration of two simple property pages.

General   The General tab (see Figure 3.12) contains the basic advertisement properties.

   Name   Enter the name of the advertisement.

   Comment   Enter a description of the advertisement's purpose.

   Package   Enter the name of the package you are advertising.

   Program   Enter the program being advertised relative to the package.

   Collection   Enter the name of the collection to which you wish to advertise.

   Include members of subcollections   Enable this selection (enabled by default) to propagate the advertisement to subcollections of the primary collection.

F I G U R E 3.12

Defining advertise-
ment properties

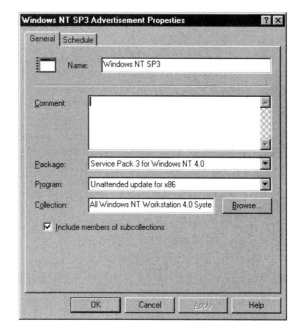

Schedule   The Schedule tab (see Figure 3.13) defines when the advertisement should become active, if it should become mandatory, and if and when
it should expire. The priority to be assigned to the advertisement when it is
being directed to child sites can also be defined here.

>   **Advertisement start time**   Enter the time and date that the advertisement
>   should become active. Use the Greenwich Mean Time option to specify
>   that the time and date are relative to Greenwich Mean Time.

>   **Mandatory Assignments**   Use this option to make the advertised pro-
>   gram mandatory to run once a date and time have been passed, or
>   following an event such as logon, logoff, or startup.

>   **Assignments are not mandatory over slow links**   Select this option to
>   prevent clients crossing slow links from being required to run the program
>   when it becomes mandatory for the collection.

>   **Allow users to run the program before it is assigned**   Select this option to
>   allow members of the collection to run the program before it becomes
>   mandatory to do so.

>   **Advertisement will expire**   Enter a date and time when the program will
>   no longer be advertised.

Priority   Specify a priority of low, medium (default), or high that the advertisement should receive when being sent to a child site.

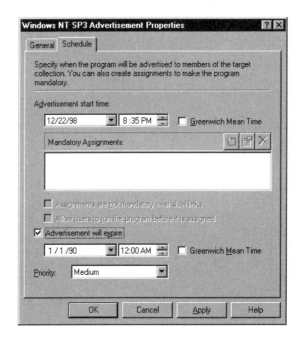

Monitoring the Software Distribution Process by Using Status Messages

The entire software distribution process can be monitored to determine the current status, including success or failure at key milestones.

Package Status and Advertisement Status provide critical information on key distribution milestones. Both of the status indicators are accessed from with the System Status section of the SMS Administrator Console.

The Package Status (see Figure 3.14) indicates the success or failure of packages' arrival at their targeted distribution points.

More verbose details of the package status can be had by viewing the associated messages.

The Advertisement Status (see Figure 3.15) displays statistics detailing the successes and failures related to the delivery of an advertisement, and those of its associated programs.

The Package Status indicates that the MS SP3 has arrived successfully at the target distribution points.

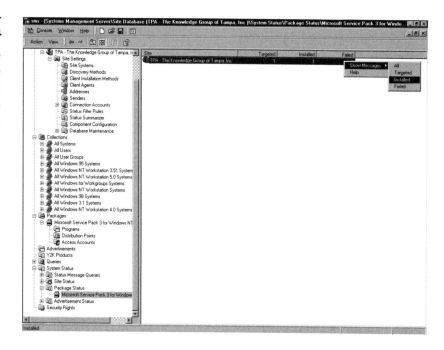

The Advertisement Status indicates that MS SP3 has not yet been received by any of its targeted resources.

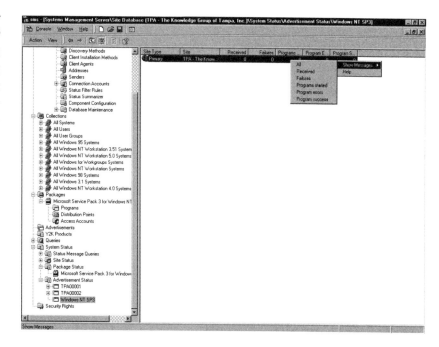

Using the SMS Client Software to Run or Install a Program on a Client Computer

When the Advertised Programs Client Agent is installed on a client, it receives two new applets in Control Panel. The applets provide the ability to initialize and monitor the installation of advertised programs on the client.

Advertised Programs   Launches the Advertised Programs Wizard, which is used to initialize advertised programs manually.

Advertised Programs Monitor   The monitor shows the status of advertised programs while they are running.

Removing Advertised Software from Distribution Points

The removal of advertised software from distribution points is performed using the Manager Distribution Points Wizard. Using the Wizard you can specify the individual distribution points from which you want to remove a given package.

In addition to the ability to remove specific packages from a distribution point, you can also discontinue the use of a system in the role of a distribution point. When the role of distribution point is removed from a system, by modifying the site system's properties, all packages held at the distribution point are removed.

Note that the removal of software from distribution points does not remove associated advertisements to clients on CAPs. It is also necessary to delete advertisements if you do not want clients attempting to install advertised packages.

Configuring and Using Software Metering

The software metering function can be used both to enforce licensing requirements and to evaluate software requirements within a organization. To use software metering properly you should know the right way to configure each component and to generate meaningful reports based on collected information.

Configuring Software Metering Servers and Client Components

The Software Metering component (see Figure 3.16) is accessed from within Component Configuration.

FIGURE 3.16

The Software Metering component is located below Component Configuration.

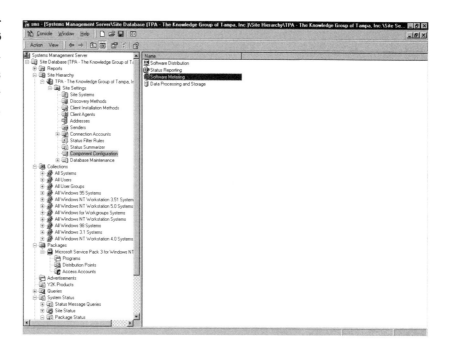

A review of the Software Metering properties page follows.

General The General tab (see Figure 3.17) controls the product name and version properties.

   Product version policy Full requires that the version of the product ran at the client match the exact same version number as the defined product to be considered a match. Partial (default) allows for partial version matching (e.g., version 1 matches 1a, 1.1, and so forth).

   Program name policy Standard (default) uses the program name shown in Windows Explorer. Original uses the name found in the executable's program header.

F I G U R E 3.17

The Software Metering components General properties page

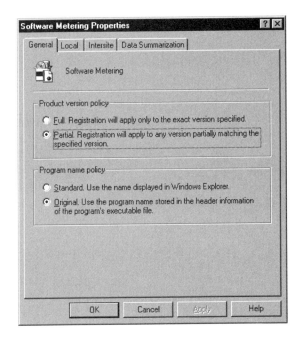

Local   The Local tab (see Figure 3.18) is used to schedule the frequency of local management functions.

> **License balancing**   Specifies when to balance licenses between a site's metering servers.
>
> **Site management**   Specifies the frequency that the list of managed software is propagated to child sites.
>
> **Data collation**   Specifies when product usage information should be moved to the site server from the software metering server.

In addition to configuring the Software Metering component, you must enable the Software Metering Client Agent.

Intersite   The Intersite tab is used to configure when unused product licenses should be transferred between sites.

Data Summarization   The Data Summarization tab is used to define the rules to be followed by SMS when summarizing software usage. Data are summarized on a scheduled basis to reduce the storage requirements at the SQL Server.

FIGURE 3.18

The Software Metering component's Local properties page

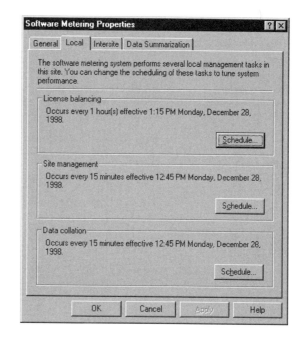

Adding Products to Be Licensed

To access the Software Metering interface (see Figure 3.19) from within the SMS Administrator Console, highlight the Site Database, select Action, and click Software Metering.

Initially, all software usage is tracked only to determine software usage. Until you specify which products require licensing, all products will be treated as if they have no licensing requirements.

You can register products by clicking on the Add Product icon in the Define Metered Software window, or by right-clicking on a product displayed in the Unlicensed tab of Software Metering Summary, and selecting register.

When you choose to choose to add a product by clicking the Add Product icon, you can elect to create a new license definition or you can import a license policy, if one is provided by the manufacturer.

The steps below detail the information you must provide or confirm when adding a new product in the New Product window (see Figure 3.20).

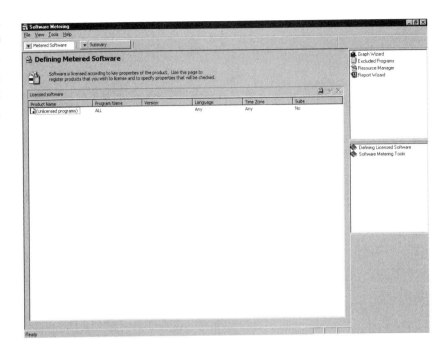

Details

The Details section includes the following entries:

Product name   Enter the name of the product for display purposes in reports.

Serial number   Enter the serial number of the product.

Purchase date   Enter the date you purchased the product.

Number of licenses   Enter a value from 0 to 2,147,483,647.

Enforce the license limits for this product   Check this box if you want the system to enforce license compliance based on the number of licenses you entered earlier.

File Details

The File Details section includes the following entries:

Program name   Enter or click the ellipse and select the name of the executable program including the file extension.

Version   Enter the product version if desired to limit license enforcement only to a specific version, otherwise it will track all versions of a given program name collectively.

Language   Enter the language version to track.

This product is a suite parent   Check this entry when registering a suite parent (e.g., Microsoft Office), but not when entering a member of the suite.

Time Zone

Enter any time zone restrictions.

Load Profile

Click on the Load Profile button to allow you to select a license profile that will provide product name, user name, computer, and time zone properties.

Configuring Licensing Options

Software metering provides more than simply an account of who used which products. You can control the use of products by restricting them to specific computers, groups, and users. You can even restrict product usage to certain times of the day.

The following sections detail the property settings accessed by double-clicking on a licensed product in Defining Metered Software.

The product (unlicensed programs) can be modified to adjust the settings for all unregistered programs that have not been excluded.

Identification

The Identification tab allows you to change basic product details including product name, number of licenses, serial number, and purchase date.

Permissions

The Permissions tab (see Figure 3.21) controls the users, groups, and computers that are allowed access to the licensed product.

F I G U R E   3.21

Controlling access to a product

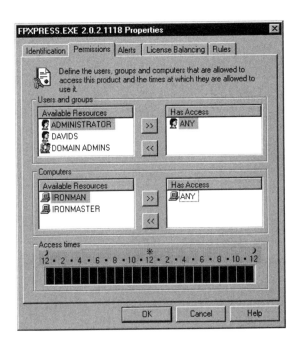

The computer, user, and group resources must first be defined using the Resource Manager.

Users and groups Only users and groups listed under Has Access will be permitted to use the licensed product.

Computers Only persons accessing the licensed product from computers listed under Has Access will receive access.

The reserved name ANY can be used to represent all users, groups, or computers.

Access times Access to the product will be granted only during the hours highlighted.

Alerts The Alerts tab (see Figure 3.22) controls which product-related events will result in an alert being issued.

Low licenses Generates an alert when the number of licenses falls below the low license threshold.

Out of licenses Generates an alert when the product is out of licenses. This is the only setting that is turned on by default.

Access denial Generates an alert based on access to the product being denied because of insufficient licenses or permissions.

Enable inactivity monitoring Lets the system determine if a product is inactive and take action to recoup the license.

Perform actions after x minutes of inactivity Enter the number of minutes that the system should wait before generating an event, showing a warning dialog box to the client, or shutting down the application.

License Balancing The License Balancing tab (see Figure 3.23) controls how the system will perform load balancing for a specific product. The entries in the following list are used by the Software Metering component when it performs license balancing at scheduled intervals.

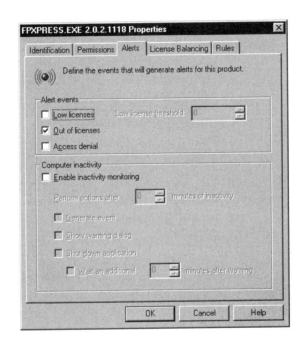

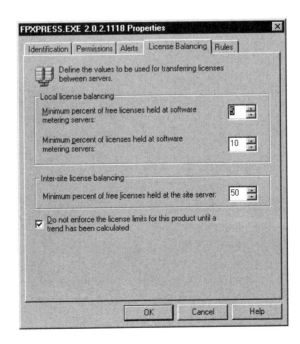

Minimum percent of free licenses held at software metering servers   Enter the percentage of available licenses that should be available at each metering server. When load balancing occurs, the system will transfer available licenses, if any, between servers so that they all have at least the preferred minimum.

Minimum percent of licenses held at software metering servers   Enter the minimum percentage of product licenses to be held at each software metering server. This prevents load balancing from removing too many licenses from a given server.

Minimum percent of free licenses held at the site server   Enter the minimum percent of available product licenses to be maintained within the site. This prevents intersite license balancing from depleting a single sites licenses.

Do not enforce the license limits for this product until a trend has been calculated   Selecting this option (default) will prevent the enforcement of licensing restrictions until the site server determines which metering servers should hold licenses based on trend calculations. This option is often unchecked in a lab environment to confirm proper enforcement of licensing restrictions, but should leave it enabled in a production environment.

Rules   The Rules tab (see Figure 3.24) controls product-specific license settings.

Enable concurrent licensing of this product   Select this option to allow a single user to request multiple licenses of the same product.

Multiple instances count as one   Select this option to charge only a single license against concurrent use of a product on the same system.

Allow license extensions (second copies)   Select this option if the product's licensing agreement allows a single user to have the product loaded in multiple locations simultaneously (i.e., home, office).

License expires   Select this option to specify a date when the license will expire.

Enforce the license limits for this product   Select this option (default) to enforce license limits. If this option is not selected the system will not issue denials based on a lack of free licenses.

Allow licenses to be checked-out for this product   Select this option if licenses will be assigned to specific computers for a duration of time. You can specify a maximum check-out time and also generate a warning message to the user before the license expires.

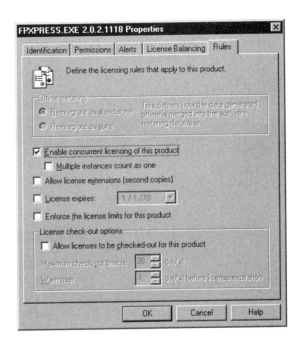

Excluding Products from Being Metered

You may want to exclude certain products from the metering process. Often the license to use a product is inherent with the operating system. For example, when you purchase a license to use Microsoft Windows 98 you are licensed to use accessory programs such as calculator and notepad.

If a product does not require licensing and/or should not be tracked by Software Metering, you should include it in the list of Excluded Programs (see Figure 3.25).

Metering Software

Much has already been said in this unit about configuring software metering components, however, it is good to review the basic metering components and system flows. The following list defines the required steps to meter software:

1. Install software metering as an optional SMS component.

F I G U R E 3.25

Excluding programs
from being metered

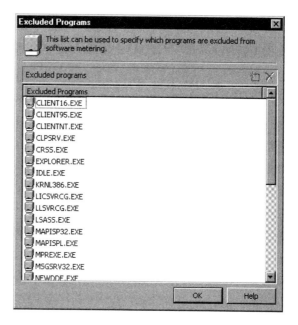

2. Assign one or more Intel-based NT Servers with SP4 to act in the software metering server role.

3. Configure the Software Metering Properties to define policy issues, task scheduling, intersite license balancing, and data summarization rules.

4. Configure and enable the software metering client agent for the site.

Remember when configuring the software metering client agent that you can elect to perform metering in either online or offline mode, depending on whether or not you force real-time license verification.

5. Define metered software using the Software Metering tool.

After performing these steps, software metering will be configured and enabled. Regardless of whether or not license usage is being enforced, the clients will report software that has been executed at their system to a metering server. Once data have been reported to a metering server by the client, reported to the site server, and passed to the SQL database, it is possible to generate reports on software usage.

Managing Software Metering Data

Obviously, software metering can generate a significant amount of data. This is compounded by the fact that metered software data is passed from child sites to parent sites. In order to control the size of the software metering databases at each site, and ultimately at the central site, you can implement data summarization. By establishing data summarization rules and schedules, the data collected about license use by each client for a given product can be merged into a single more generalized entry.

Generating Reports and Graphs

Software Metering includes a Report Wizard that can be used to generate reports and graphs on numerous aspects, including:

- Detailed Product Use (Grouped by Product)
- Detailed Product Use (Grouped by User)
- Unlicensed Program Usage

The Report Wizard will generate the desired report to the screen; then you have the option of printing it. Although this objective deals specifically with generating reports and graphs based on software metering data, it also lends itself to a discussion of some general topics related to Crystal Info.

The fact that the SMS database is housed on Microsoft SQL Server opens up several reporting options. Although it is possible to query the SQL database directly, this is not recommended. A majority of reporting will be done using Crystal Info, which is included with SMS 2.

Crystal Info for SMS is an SMS-specific version of the fully featured product, Seagate Crystal Info version 6. It is included with SMS in order to create, modify, schedule, and run reports using data from the SMS site database. Crystal Info uses the WBEM Source (WBEM ODBC) driver to connect to the SMS database and expose the classes and properties for reporting.

The creation or designing of Crystal Info reports is outside the scope of this book, but you should familiarize yourself with certain key elements. The following list details some of these items:

- Reports can be saved either with or without data. When a report is saved without data, the person viewing the report must have rights to access the underlying objects. To specify your credentials when running a report, select Database, Log On Server, and WBEM Source;

then provide your logon properties. This can also be done from the Accounts tab when scheduling a report.

- Reports can be sent to colleagues in other sites, or even to organizations, who can then run the reports against their own SMS databases. To direct the report query to their database, they must select the option Database, Set Location.

- In order for a report to be executed and the query to run, you must schedule the report. Reports can be scheduled to run immediately or at a given time; the recurrence pattern can then be set so that the report will be automatically updated.

In order to be fully prepared for the exam, you should try to create, schedule, and modify a basic report that returns results similar to those of the SQL and WQL queries discussed earlier.

Crystal Info uses three services: Info Agent, Info APS, and Info Sentinel. Running reports is dependent on the Info APS service available. If it fails to run successfully on your system, you might try adding NM to the list of its dependencies in the registry under the Info APS key.

Configuring Software and Hardware Inventory Collection for a Site

1. Resources must be _____ prior to being available for inventory collection.

2. Hardware inventory configuration is performed on a per _____ basis.

3. Hardware inventory configuration changes are made by adjusting the properties of the _____ agent.

4. True/False: You can control the frequency with which inventory should be updated.

5. True /False: Hardware Inventory is performed only for 32-bit Windows-based clients.

6. True/False: Clients report collected information directly to the site server.

7. The simple schedule allows inventory to be collected on a schedule of _____, _____, or _____.

8. To specify the inventory should occur on a particular day of the week or month, you need to use the _____ schedule.

9. When the hardware inventory agent is installed on 32-bit systems, the %Windir%\ MS\SMS\Clicomp_____ directory is created.

10. The SMS_def.mof file is compiled by _____ to configure the CIMOM schema.

STUDY QUESTIONS

11. _____ is the executable run on 32-bit clients to collect and store inventory.

12. When complete inventory is being reported, `Hinv32.exe` creates a _____ file.

13. When a partial inventory is being reported, `Hinv32.exe` creates a _____ file.

14. The software inventory agent requires that clients have a minimum of _____ MB of available virtual memory and at least _____ MB of free disk space.

15. By default, only files ending in _____ will be inventoried.

16. True/False: Wildcard statements such as *.* are convenient ways of identifying all files that should be inventoried.

17. True/False: You can limit the amount of megabytes collected in a single inventory cycle.

18. True/False: File collection is the process of moving files from a client to the site server via a client access point.

19. In general, file collection requires approximately _____ percent of a client's drive to be free space.

Managing Inventory Data

20. The _____ is used to view collected inventory from within the Systems Management Server Console.

21. The default inventory schema is loaded into CIMOM from the _____ file.

22. The SMS_def.mof file contains all of the necessary categories to make SMS _____ - compliant.

23. True/False: IDMIFs can be used to add both additional architectures and property classes.

24. True/False: IDMIFs and NOIDMIFs are used as a replacement to the default SMS_def.mof.

25. NOIDMIFs are used to extend the hardware inventory _____ for specific clients.

Distributing Software

26. The _____ program is included with SMS to simplify the creation of installation scripts.

27. When using SMS Installer the baseline system is referred to as the _____ server.

28. When using SMS Installer, the systems you deploy packages to are called _____ computers.

29. True/False: The SMS Installer can only be installed on a site server.

30. True/False: Packages to be distributed using SMS require a package definition file from the manufacturer.

31. Which Data Source option should be selected when the application defined by a package is already installed at the clients?

32. Which Data Source option should be select when the source media may not be available at a later time?

33. What name would be created for the default package share on logical drive D?

34. The default sending priority assigned to packages is _____.

35. True/False: A preferred sender must be assigned in order to transfer packages to a child site.

36. A _____ defines the set of commands to be executed by a client for a specific package.

37. The location of a program's command line executable can be defined by setting the _____ parameter.

38. When a program requires a specific action such as restarting the computer, this action can be entered as the _____ parameter.

39. When a collection consists of dissimilar hardware platforms that are not all capable of running a program being distributed to it, the _____ parameter can be used to limit which members of the collection will execute the advertised program.

STUDY QUESTIONS

40. The default setting for the program Environment setting, Program can run, is set to

_____.

41. An _____ must be created to make clients aware of a program.

42. True/False: By default, advertisements directed to a collection are also sent to its subcollections.

43. True/False: Assigned programs (those made mandatory) that have not yet been executed must always be run once the assigned date and time have been passed.

44. When clients located in multiple time zones should run a program simultaneously, the start time should be set relative to _____.

45. True/False: In order to receive advertisements, a system must be a member of a collection and have the Advertised Programs Client Agent installed.

46. True/False: When a collection is based on a query, re-executing the query updates the collection.

47. True/False: The Package Status indicates the successful arrival or failure of packages to targeted clients.

48. A client can initialize advertised programs manually by launching the

_____.

49. When advertising service packs, you should ensure that the program can run with _____ rights.

50. Deleting an advertisement removes it from both _____ and _____.

51. True/False: Deleting an advertisement does not affect the associated program.

Configuring and Using Software Metering

52. The primary tool included with SMS 2 for creating reports is _____.

53. In order for a Crystal Info report to run or be updated it must be _____.

54. True/False: Crystal Info reports can be run only against the database against which they were originally created.

55. True/False: By default, software metering would consider software product versions 1a, 1b, and 1c as a match with version 1.

56. License balancing balances licenses between a site's _____ servers.

57. The transfer of unused product licenses between sites is configured under the _____ tab of Software Metering properties.

58. Valid entries for the Number of Licenses entry in the Details tab are between _____ and 2,147,483,647.

59. True/False: When metering products such as Microsoft Excel and Microsoft Word, you should specify the option This Product Is a Suite Parent.

60. Before controlling access to licenses based on computer, user, or group names, you must define them using _____.

61. The reserved name _____ can be used to represent all users, groups, or computers within Resource Manager.

62. True/False: Access to products can be restricted in Resource Manager based on time of day or day of week.

63. True/False: By default, license limits are not enforced until a trend has been calculated.

64. True/False: Denials based on a lack of free licenses can be disabled on a per product basis.

65. Products that are licensed with the operating system or do not require licensing limits should be included in the _____ list.

66. Software Metering reports can be generated using the _____.

SAMPLE TEST

3-1 Which of the following statements about hardware inventory collection is true?

    A. Hardware inventory is enabled on a per domain basis.

    B. Hardware inventory is enabled on a per site basis.

    C. Hardware inventory is performed only on 32-bit clients.

    D. Hardware inventory is performed only on 16-bit clients.

3-2 Which of the steps should the administrator perform to extend the hardware properties reported on an individual client?

    A. Enable additional properties in the `SMS_def.mof`.

    B. Create a NOIDMIF and install it on the client.

    C. Create an IDMIF and install it on the client.

    D. Create an IDMIF and install it on the site server.

3-3 The Example Company administrator has deleted a client using the SMS Administrator Console but has not yet removed the SMS client software from the client.

At the next scheduled hardware inventory the client generates a `Hinv32.hid` file and passes it to a client access point.

What will occur when the site server tries to process the `Hinv32.hid` file?

    A. The mismatched record will corrupt the SMS database.

    B. The mismatched record will initiate resynchronization.

    C. The mismatched record will result in the primary site server directing the client to remove the SMS client software.

    D. The mismatched record will be placed in the `Badmifs` directory at the primary site server.

SAMPLE TEST

3-4 Which of the following statements regarding software inventory collection are correct?

  A. Software inventory occurs on the same schedule as that defined for hardware inventory collection.

  B. Clients require a minimum of 3MB of available virtual memory.

  C. Clients require a minimum of 2MB of free disk space.

  D. By default, only files ending in `.exe` or `.com` are inventoried.

3-5 The Example Company administrator wants to force all clients to run a copy of a virus protection program that is already installed on their systems.

Which of the following steps should the administrator perform?

  A. Create a new package and specify **This package doesn't contain any files** in the Distribution Settings tab.

  B. Create a new package and specify **This package doesn't contain any files** in the Data Source tab.

  C. Create a new package and specify **This package doesn't contain any files** in the Data Access tab.

  D. Create a new package and specify **Always obtain file from source directory** in the Data Source tab.

  E. Click on the **Update** button in the Data Source tab.

3-6 Which of the following priorities is the sending priority assigned by default to a new package?

  A. Low.

  B. Medium.

  C. High.

  D. No default priority is assigned.

3-7   Which of the following statements is true regarding program advertisements?

    A. Start times are always entered relative to Greenwich Mean Time.

    B. By default, advertisements are assigned a priority of low.

    C. By default, advertisements are assigned a priority of medium.

    D. By default, advertisements expire 30 days after being issued.

3-8   Which of the following statements about the SMS Installer are correct?

    A. The SMS Installer is used to create packages.

    B. The SMS Installer is used to create and distribute packages.

    C. Reference computers must run Microsoft Windows NT.

    D. Windows 3.*x*–based computers can be reference servers.

UNIT

4

Integration and
Interoperability

Test Objectives

- **Install and configure an SMS client computer.**

  - Discover client computers.

  - Configure client installation methods for client computers.

  - Run the client computer installation.

  - Identify changes made to client computers.

- **Install and configure remote utilities on client computers.**

  - Configure Remote Tools Client Agent at the site server.

  - Configure Remote Tools settings at the client computer.

  - Configure protocols on client computers.

  - Use diagnostic utilities for client computers.

  - Use Remote Tools.

- **Install and configure Windows NT Event to SNMP Trap translator.**

- **Install and configure Health Monitor to monitor Windows NT Server computers.**

 Exam objectives are subject to change at any time without prior notice and at Microsoft's sole discretion. Please visit Microsoft's Training and Certification Web site (www.microsoft.com/Train_Cert/) for the most current listing of exam objectives.

This unit will detail some of the key areas of SMS management, including the installation and configuration of clients and the proper use of remote control utilities.

Installing and Configuring an SMS Client Computer

This section reviews the discovery process and the key issues you face when preparing for and performing SMS client installation.

Discovering Client Computers

Discovery is the process by which an organization's resources are exposed to SMS. The types of resources that can be discovered are not limited to client computers, but rather include servers, network devices, and Windows NT groups and users.

The concept of discovering resources did not exist in earlier versions of SMS. In the past, SMS client software had to be installed on a resource in order for the resource to be identified. Now, however, resources can be listed in the database even if they don't have SMS client software installed. Discovery of resources and client installation are independent processes, but the discovery of resources is usually done with the intent of next installing client software. The available discovery methods are discussed in the sections that follow.

Windows Networking Logon Discovery

It is reasonable to expect that the use of Microsoft NT will be prevalent in organizations implementing SMS. Enabling Windows Networking Logon

Discovery allows you to collect and collate resource information based on which NT domain's clients are validated.

The Windows Networking Logon Discovery is configured using the settings described in the next sections.

General The General tab (see Figure 4.1) is used to configure the following:

Enable Windows Networking Logon Discovery Selecting this check box enables this discovery method.

Keep logon point lists for discovery and installation synchronized Selecting this check box ensures that adding or removing domains as logon points is reflected both here and in the Windows Networking Logon Client Installation logon points lists. If you elect not to use this option, you will not be assured that all potential clients that are discovered will be installed as SMS clients.

Logon Points Enter the names of NT domains for which you want to discover clients. Take special care when using domains that may span multiple subnets, as is often the case in the Master Domain model.

F I G U R E 4.1

The General properties of Windows Networking Logon Discovery

Logon Settings   The Logon Settings tab (see Figure 4.2) is used to control the following properties:

Modify user logon scripts   This option must remain enabled in order to allow SMS to automatically modify logon scripts to call `smsls.bat`. If a logon script is not specified in a user's profile, SMS will direct it to `smsls.bat`. If the client has a preexisting logon script it will be modified to call `smsls.bat`.

Location to insert script changes   This specifies whether SMS should place the call to `smsls.bat` at the top or bottom of preexisting logon scripts.

FIGURE 4.2

The Logon Settings properties of Windows Networking Logon Discovery

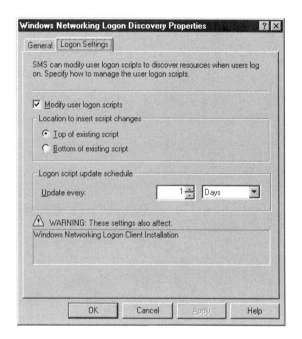

Windows NT supports the use of executable (i.e., .exe) files as user logon scripts. If a client's logon script is neither a .bat nor a .cmd file, it cannot be modified automatically.

Logon script update schedule   This specifies the logon script update interval in number of hours, days, or weeks.

NetWare Bindery Server Logon Discovery

The term *bindery server* is used here to refer to Novell's NetWare servers, versions 3.11 and 3.12. NetWare Bindery is Novell's older flat database. This method of discovery causes all clients who run the server's system logon script to be recorded as resources.

Configuration of NetWare Bindery Server Logon Discovery involves setting the following options:

General   The General tab (see Figure 4.3) includes the following options:

Enable NetWare Bindery Logon Discovery   Selecting this check box enables this discovery method.

Keep logon point lists for discovery and installation synchronized   Selecting this check box ensures that adding or removing NetWare 3.*x* servers as logon points is reflected both here and in the NetWare Bindery Server Client Installation logon points list. If you elect not to use this option you will not be assured that all potential clients that are discovered will be installed as SMS clients.

Logon points   Enter the names of the NetWare 3.*x* servers for which you want clients to be discovered.

F I G U R E   4.3

The General properties of NetWare Bindery Server Logon Discovery

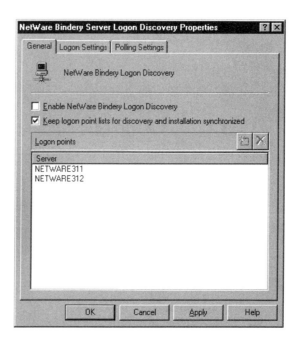

Logon Settings The Logon Settings tab (see Figure 4.4) is used to control the following properties:

Modify login scripts This option is required to let SMS modify the system logon scripts (net$log.dat) on servers used as logon points.

Location to insert script changes Specify whether SMS should place the call to smsls.bat at the top or bottom of an existing system login script.

Microsoft uses the term *logon script* to refer to a script executed during the logon process, whereas Novell calls their process the "login process" so Novell uses the term *login script*.

The keyword EXIT is often used within conditional statements in the system login script. If a client executes the EXIT function before reaching the call to smsls.bat, the smsls.bat batch file will not be executed.

Logon point update schedule Specify the login script update interval in hours, days, or weeks.

Polling Settings Because NetWare servers will not actively run a reporting service, the site server must periodically collect the discovery data records (DDRs) placed by clients at client access points (CAPs) on NetWare servers.

The polling settings have only a single setting (DDR polling schedule), which controls the frequency in hours, days, or weeks that the site server connects to CAPs on NetWare servers to collect DDRs.

NetWare NDS Logon Discovery

NetWare Directory Services (NDS) Logon Discovery is used to discover clients of NetWare 4.*x* and 5.*x* systems. NDS is significantly more flexible in its approach to object management than were the bindery-based versions that preceded it. Rather than having a single system login script, with NDS there is the possibility of multiple container login scripts per server. If the NDS context of the user's account being validated is the same as that of a container with a login script, then the script will be executed. This means that even with a single server you may need to enter multiple logon points, depending on where accounts will be located in the NDS tree.

FIGURE 4.4

The Logon Settings
properties of NetWare
Bindery Server Logon
Discovery

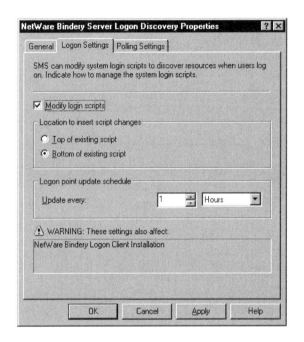

When using NDS Logon Discovery, container objects, rather than individual servers, are entered in the Logon Point list.

The settings are identical to those of NetWare Bindery Logon Discovery, with the exception that container objects, not individual servers, are entered as logon points.

Network Discovery

Network Discovery may easily be considered the most complex of the discovery methods. The complexity comes from the need to configure both the scope in which discovery should be performed and the level of component detail desired.

For a resource to be discovered using Network Discovery it must have an IP address.

The Network Discovery properties are defined by seven interrelated tabs, which are outlined in the next sections.

General   The General tab (see Figure 4.5) provides access to the following options:

Enable network discovery   Selecting this check box enables this discovery method.

Type of discovery   Specify the level of detail that you want to be returned by the network discovery process. The options include:

- *Topology*. This selection returns only information on the network topology for the site. Select this option to populate the site database with the information (routers, subnets) necessary for Network Trace to diagram the relationship between site systems.

- *Topology and client*. In addition to the information gathered by selecting the previous option, this selection also collects the names and addresses of potential clients. Select this option, in conjunction with Remote Client Installation, to push SMS client software to NT systems.

- *Topology, client, and client operating system*. In addition to the information gathered by selecting the previous option, this selection collects operating system information about each of the potential clients. Select this option to determine the number and type of potential resources before initiating any means of SMS client installation.

Slow network   Select this option if you will be requesting resource information from Simple Network Management Protocol (SNMP) devices located across slow networks.

WARNING   Be careful when selecting Remote Client Installation. You might not want SMS to push SMS client software to all your NT systems.

Subnets   It is possible to contain the area of a network in which resources will be discovered by configuring subnets to search. The discovery process will be restricted to operation within the defined subnets.

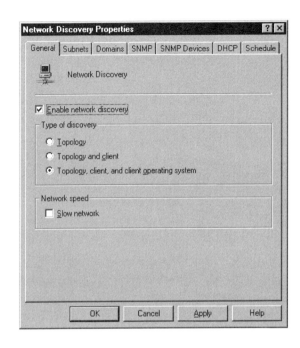

Domains   It is often convenient to identify a logical area of a network where resources should be discovered by configuring domains to search. The discovery process will poll the systems returned from browsers in the listed domains.

SNMP   Network Discovery can take advantage of information collected already by devices (e.g., routers) using SNMP. The following options are set at the SNMP tab:

   Community name   Enter at least one SNMP-read community name. The discovery process will extract information from the devices in the community in order to determine subnets and identify routers.

   Hop count   This option controls the number of hops across routers that will be allowed by the discovery process. By default the hop count is 0, meaning only devices on the local subnet will be interrogated. Every time you go across a router, that is considered one hop. Use caution when entering this value, as you'll want to control the range of discovery across your wide area network (WAN).

SNMP Devices Network Discovery can be configured to extract information from specific SNMP-enabled hardware by listing them by either name or IP address in the SNMP Devices list.

By identifying the devices manually, the Network Discovery process can often determine additional information.

DHCP When dynamic host configuration protocol (DHCP) is being used on a network, it is possible to specify the DHCP servers from which to extract IP information about resources.

Schedule The Schedule tab is used to set the frequency with which Network Discovery should be performed. Depending on the options configured, the process could become relatively bandwidth intensive. This option allows you to schedule discovery to occur during nonpeak hours.

Heartbeat Discovery

Heartbeat Discovery is used to reconfirm the existence of resources initially discovered by other means. Resources cannot be discovered initially by Heartbeat Discovery. Enable this discovery method if you will have many resources that do not have active users. This method is important because SMS runs an automated task to clean out resources that have not been updated for the past 90 days (default).

From this tab, you can elect to enable or disable Heartbeat Discovery and establish a recurring schedule.

Windows Networking User Group Discovery

This method of discovery is used to gather the names of NT groups used within a domain. The process works by polling domain controllers in the domains listed as logon points.

Windows Networking User Account Discovery

This method of discovery is used to gather the names of NT users used within a domain. The process works by polling domain controllers in the domains listed as logon points.

Although discovery and installation are related, they are independent processes that do not directly rely on one another; either process can be enabled independent of the other.

Whether discovered resources are classified as members of a particular site depends on the site assignment rules. A site is composed of one or more TCP/IP subnets or IPX network numbers. Only resources located within the boundaries of qualifying subnets are assigned as members of the site.

Regardless of whether a resource will be assimilated into a site, if the discovered resource contains a Windows-based operating system it will receive a copy of the SMS control panel applet. The presence of this applet does not in itself mean that client software has been installed.

Remember that it is possible for multiple sites to contain one or more of the same subnets. It is therefore possible for a client to be discovered and listed as a resource within multiple sites.

Besides the forms of discovery we've already discussed, there is one more form of discovery that is managed automatically by SMS, called Server Discovery. This method of discovery is used exclusively to collect resource information from SMS site systems and to initiate the installation of client software on them. This method is mandatory and nonconfigurable.

Configuring Client Installation Methods for Client Computers

In order for you to convert personal computer and server resources to SMS clients, you have to configure the client installation methods properly. SMS provides five ways to initialize client installation.

You can specify that the logon points should be kept in sync between Logon Discovery and Logon Installation methods. This ensures that clients are installed where they are shown as discovered resources.

Each installation method is suited for a specific situation, as described here.

Windows Networking Logon Client Installation   This method directs clients being validated within a domain listed in Logon Points to invoke the installation process by calling the `smsls.bat` logon script.

Windows NT Remote Client Installation   This method is used to install SMS client software on NT systems identified by Network Discovery or other resource discovery methods to be Windows NT servers. Be careful of this method since it can automatically install SMS Client software on all NT systems that are discovered.

NDS Server Logon Client Installation   This installation method modifies the logon scripts associated with specific NDS container objects. Once enabled, SMS client software will be installed on all clients that process the container logon script.

NetWare Bindery Server Logon Client Installation   This installation method modifies the system logon scripts on selected bindery-based servers. Once enabled, SMS client software will be installed by all clients that process the system logon script.

Manual Client Installation   This installation method is used when clients manually execute the smsman.exe (for 32-bit clients) or smsman16.exe (for 16-bit clients) program. Both programs are located by default in the directory \SMSLOGON\x86.bin\00000409. In previous versions of SMS, Windows 95 was considered a 16-bit client, but with SMS 2 Windows 95 and Windows 98 are considered 32-bit clients, so they would run smsman.exe.

Manual Client Installation is also referred to as Manual Client Discovery. This is because discovery does not have to precede the installation and because upon execution the client is listed as a discovered resource.

Running the Client Computer Installation

The installation of SMS clients will be invoked differently depending on the installation method you select. Some of the key factors that should be considered when determining which installation method to choose are detailed in the next sections.

Identifying Changes Made to Client Computers

When client installation is complete, you will note the creation of the %WinDir%\MS\SMS directory and its various subdirectories. The number of subdirectories will vary, based on which client agents were chosen to be installed.

The sample client used in this unit, IRONMASTER, has the following subdirectories below %WinDir%\MS\SMS:

- Clicomp

- Core

- IDMIFs

- NOIDMIFs

- Logs

- Sitefile

After client installation, you should verify that the proper Control Panel applets appear. In the case of IRONMASTER, these include:

- Advertised Programs: Used to launch advertised programs.

- Advertised Programs Monitor: Used to monitor the status of advertised programs as they are running.

- Remote Control: Used to configure the Remote Control options.

Additionally, the SMS control panel applet will appear but as a result of discovery not installation. This applet provides clients with the means of viewing settings including, SMS unique ID, assigned site(s), component status, and traveling mode.

Traveling mode addresses the problem of computers that are often physically moved between subnets being assigned inaccurately to multiple sites. Before a computer in traveling mode can be installed in a new site, the user will be given the option of whether or not to join the new site.

Installing and Configuring Remote Utilities on Client Computers

The remote utilities are among the most important management features provided by SMS. Using remote utilities allows you to resolve a wide range of client issues without being physically present at the client's system; even via 28.8 remote access service (RAS) connections. This section will detail how to configure the Remote Tools Client Agent, customize remote control settings, configure supporting client protocols, and use remote diagnostics and Remote Tools.

Remote Tools can be used only in conjunction with the following Microsoft Windows-based clients:

- Windows 3.*x*
- Windows 95
- Windows 98
- Windows NT Server 3.51 and above
- Windows NT Workstation 3.51 and above

Although the functions of the tools are fairly simple to understand, you should be aware of a few key configuration issues.

Configuring Remote Tools Client Agent at the Site Server

Before you can use any of the Remote Tools, the Remote Tools Client Agent has to be configured and enabled for the target systems. As with all client agents, the Remote Tools Client Agent settings are accessed from within the Client Agents section under Site Settings. With SMS 2 we can now change the options on the client without having to go to each client on the network. Double-clicking on the Remote Tools Client Agent brings up the properties window.

The Remote Tools Client Agent properties window provides a series of five tabs that are used to detail configuration choices. The next sections provide an overview of the various property groupings.

General   The General tab (see Figure 4.6) defines the basic properties, as listed here.

Enable remote tools on clients   Select this option to enable the Remote Tools Client Agent on all supported systems within the site.

Clients cannot change Policy or Notification settings   Select this option to prevent clients from modifying Policy or Notification settings through the Remote Control applet in Control Panel.

Security   The Security tab (see Figure 4.7) defines which users and groups will be able to access Windows NT clients with Remote Tools.

Administrators   Enter the names of the Windows NT users and/or Global groups that will be granted permission to access Windows NT clients.

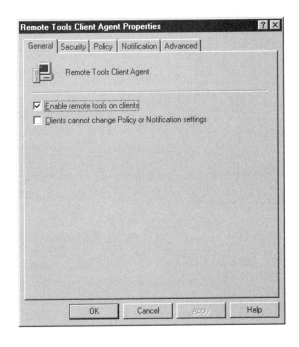

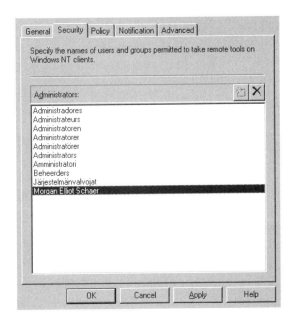

Policy   The Policy tab (see Figure 4.8) defines the default settings to be applied when the Remote Tools Client Agent is first installed.

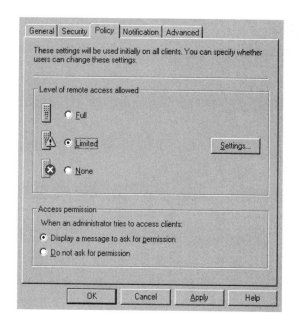

F I G U R E   4.8

The Policy properties
of the Remote Tools
Client Agent

Level of remote access   Specify the level of permissions as Full, Limited, or None.

When the permission level is specified as limited you can allow or deny each of the following capabilities:

- View client screen and control its keyboard and mouse

- Run commands on client computer

- Transfer files to and from client computer

- Restart client computer

- Exchange text messages with client (chat)

- View client computer configuration

WARNING   When conflicting permissions are specified for clients of multiple sites, the most restrictive set of permissions has precedence.

Access permission   This specifies whether the user should be prompted to permit or deny remote access attempts.

Notification   The Notification tab (see Figure 4.9) specifies if and how clients should be informed that a remote session to their system is active.

FIGURE 4.9

The Notification
properties of the
Remote Tools
Client Agent

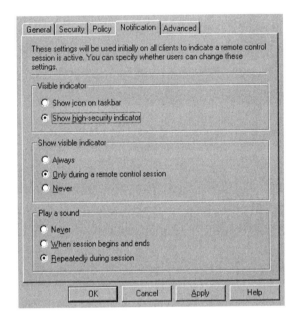

Visible indicator   This specifies which type of visual notification to give a client during a session. Select to show either an icon on the taskbar or a high-security indicator on the desktop.

Show visible indicator   This specifies when the visible indicator should appear: Always, Only During a Remote Session, or Never.

Play a sound   This specifies if or when a sound should be played: Never, When Session Begins and Ends, or Repeatedly During Session.

Advanced   The Advanced tab (see Figure 4.10) defines the advanced settings that will be applied to new clients.

Default compression for remote control   This specifies the default compression that should be used when transferring data during remote control sessions.

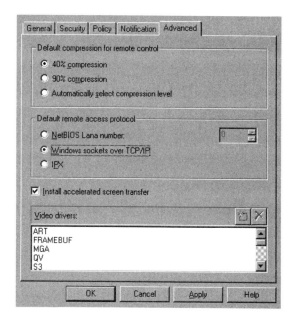

F I G U R E 4.10

The Advanced
properties of the
Remote Tools
Client Agent

Default remote access protocol   This specifies the default protocol to
which clients should bind the remote tools client agent.

Install accelerated screen transfer driver   Select the check box to use
accelerated screen transfer for clients with support video drivers installed.

Configuring Remote Tools Settings at the Client Computer

When the remote control settings configured for the site allow, clients can
customize remote control preferences using the Remote Control applet in
Control Panel.

The Remote Control applet allows users to specify local settings that
differ from those configured in the Policy and Notification tabs described
earlier. However, if the administrator elected to select the option Clients
Cannot Change Policy or Notification Settings for the Remote Tools Client
Agent, the client will be able to view but not modify the settings.

Configuring Protocols on Client Computers

The Remote Tools Client Agent is bound only to a single protocol on the
client system. In an environment with a single protocol in common and in

use exclusively on both the client and the administrative systems (i.e., TCP/IP), this is not an issue. However, when clients do not have protocols in common with those of the administrative system, or when the protocols in common are not supported by the network's routers, problems can arise.

The Advanced tab of the Remote Tools Client Agent properties page allows you to specify which client protocol the agent should bind to by default. Three protocol options are provided:

- NetBIOS Lana number (NetBEUI)
- Windows sockets over TCP/IP (default)
- IPX

Problems will occur in establishing remote sessions when the Remote Tools Client Agent is bound to a protocol that is not configured on the administrative system. In general, you should choose the protocol that is most widely used in your client base. However, the physical network topology may require you to choose a protocol such as TCP/IP or IPX over NetBIOS Lana number (commonly used with NetBEUI) because of routing limitations.

Using Diagnostic Utilities for Client Computers

Included with the remote utilities are diagnostics for both Windows NT and Windows 3.*x* systems.

Windows NT Diagnostics   Access to the Windows NT Diagnostics (see Figure 4.11) utility is gained by right-clicking on a Windows NT–based system within a collection and selecting Microsoft Windows NT Diagnostics.

The diagnostic program provides read-only details of the following areas:

Version   Windows NT version and service pack number, plus registered user information

System settings   Hardware platform and processor descriptions

Display   Video adapter settings and driver details

Services   Status of client services and devices

Resources   IRQ assignments

Environment   Environment variable names and values

Network   General, Transport protocols, Settings, and Statistics

F I G U R E   4.11

Viewing the Windows
NT Diagnostics for
IRONMASTER

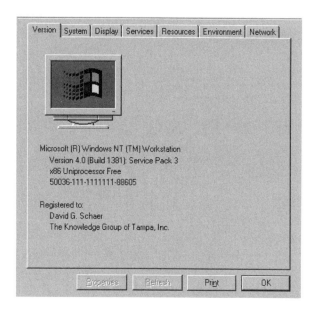

Windows 3.x   Windows 3.x clients cannot be accessed using the Windows
NT Diagnostics utility. However, special Windows 3.x diagnostic tools become
available when the focus of Remote Tools is set to a Windows 3.x client.

The following listing provides the names of the Windows 3.x categories
that can be examined:

- Windows Memory
- Windows Modules
- Windows Tasks
- Windows Classes
- Windows Heap Walk
- GDI Heap Walk
- CMOS Info
- Device Drivers
- ROM Info
- Interrupt Vectors
- DOS Memory Map

Using Remote Tools

Remote Tools are a collection of functions that can be used to effectively administer a remote client. A brief description of each tool and its usage is provided here.

Remote Control   Use this tool to take remote control of a client machine.

Reboot   Use this tool to force a reboot of the remote client.

Chat   Use this tool to establish a chat session between the administrative system and a client.

File Transfer   Use this tool to transfer files to a remote client.

Remote Execute   Use this tool to remotely launch a file on a remote client.

Ping Test   Use this tool to test the communication link between the administrative system and the client. This is not the same Ping program as commonly used with TCP/IP and is not TCP/IP dependent.

Additionally, several diagnostics noted previously can be executed when remotely accessing Windows 3.*x* clients.

Installing and Configuring Windows NT Event to SNMP Trap Translator

The Event to Trap Translator (see Figure 4.12) monitors the Windows NT Event log on Windows NT clients. When events of a specific type or ID are located, they are translated into SNMP trap messages. The trap messages are then forwarded on by the SNMP service to a specified trap destination.

Although it is possible to view the Event Log of each Windows NT client individually, the Event to Trap Translator provides a means of actively monitoring for specific events and reporting them to a central location.

The Event to Trap Translator functions only on Windows NT clients where TCP/IP is installed and the SNMP agent is running and configured to forward traps.

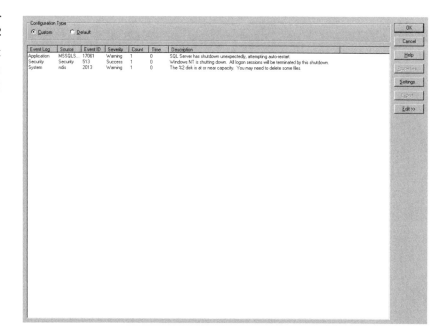

FIGURE 4.12

Configuring the Event
to Trap Translator on
IRONMAN

The Event IDs that the Event to Trap Translator monitors for can be selected from Event Sources. The Event Sources are broken into the three categories of Application, Security, and System, based on the Event Log to which they report. For example, MSSQLSERVER is located in the Application category. When MSSQLSERVER is selected as the event source, a list of associated events is loaded from a message file. Any event that is then selected will be among those for which traps will be generated.

Microsoft Windows NT provides only an SNMP agent. Traps must be reported to systems running a third-party SNMP manager (e.g., HP OpenView).

Installing and Configuring Health Monitor to Monitor Windows NT Server Computers

Healthmon is composed of both a client-side agent and an MMC snap-in console. Using the HealthMon console (see Figure 4.13), you can monitor the status of numerous components of Windows NT 4 and of Back-Office applications including SQL Server, IIS Server, Exchange Server, SNA Server, and SMS.

FIGURE 4.13

Monitoring the status
of components using
HealthMon

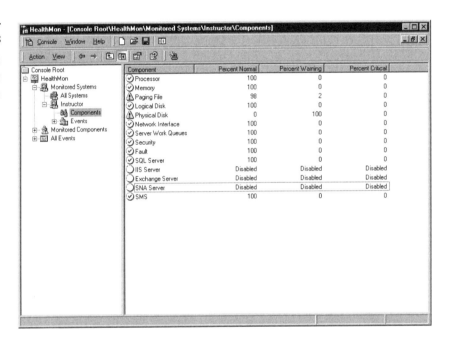

When monitoring NT components, you can specify threshold limits for properties of the following components:

- Processor
- Memory
- Paging File
- Logical Disk

- Physical Disk

- Network Interface

- Server Work Queues

- Security

- Fault

 For the Healthmon Agent to accurately report status of certain components you will need to enable the required counters. For example, before enabling physical disk monitoring, you must enable the disk performance counters by running Diskperf.

In order for the Healthmon agent to accurately report data back to the Healthmon Console, performance monitor counters for each of the monitored components must be enabled at the monitored system. If data for a specific component are not reported, the Healthmon Console will evaluate the component as being in a warning state 100 percent of the time.

Installing and Configuring an SMS Client Computer

1.   True/False: Network Discovery can only locate resources that have an IP address.

2.   True/False: The discovery process is responsible for installing client software on client computers and servers it identifies.

3.   True/False: Only resources that have SMS client software installed will be listed in the resource collections.

4.   When configuring Windows Networking Logon Discovery, you must enter the names of _____ as Logon Points.

5.   To ensure that the logon points specified in Windows Networking Logon Discovery are identical to those of Windows Networking Logon Client Installation, you should select the option _____.

6.   True/False: A single NT domain can span multiple subnets.

7.   True/False: SMS can modify all logon scripts supported by Windows NT clients to call the smsls.bat file.

8.   If a user profile does not specify a logon script, Windows Networking Logon Discovery can direct it to the _____ file.

9.   Novell NetWare versions _____ and _____ are supported by NetWare Bindery Server Logon Discovery.

10.   When configuring NetWare Bindery Server Logon Discovery, you must enter the names of _____ as logon points.

11.   True/False: You can configure the schedule with which NetWare servers will report collected discovery information to the site server.

12.   _____ refers to the discovery information collected from a resource.

13.   NetWare Bindery Logon Discovery modifies the _____ logon script, net$log.dat.

14.   True/False: NetWare NDS Logon Discovery modifies the system logon script in order that all validated clients are discovered as resources.

15.   When configuring NetWare NDS Logon Discovery, you must enter the names of _____ as logon points.

16.   True/False: Regardless of the type of discovery selected, Network Discovery will always identify routers and subnets.

17.   When requesting resource information from SNMP devices located across a slow link, you can select the _____ option to increase the SNMP timeout values.

18. Network Discovery is often used in conjunction with the _____ method of client installation.

19. When configured to identify resources within a domain, system names to poll will be retrieved from _____ in the domain.

20. The default SNMP community name is _____.

21. What is default hop count specified in SNMP properties?

22. When the hop count is set to zero, only resources on the local _____ will be discovered.

23. SNMP devices from which to extract information can be identified by either _____ or _____.

24. True/False: Network Discovery can be configured to extract IP address information for resources from DHCP servers.

25. _____ is used to reconfirm existence of resources discovered by other means.

26. True/False: Heartbeat Discovery occurs continuously and therefore is not configured to run at scheduled intervals.

27. _____ is used to discover NT groups by querying domain controllers.

28. _____ is used to discover NT users by querying domain controllers.

29. True/False: The presence of the SMS Control Panel applet confirms that all SMS client software is installed.

30. True/False: It is possible for clients to be discovered and listed as resources in multiple sites.

31. Manual Client Installation is initiated by executing the _____ file for Windows NT clients.

32. Manual Client Installation is initiated by executing the _____ file for Windows 16-bit clients.

33. True/False: When NetWare NDS Server Logon Client Installation is enabled, SMS client software will be installed on all clients of the NetWare NDS server.

34. By default, the SMS client software is installed in
`\%WinDir%\`_____`\`_____.

35. True/False: After installing the SMS client software, the following applets will always appear in Control Panel: Advertised Programs, Advertised Programs Monitor, and Remote Control.

36. True/False: Only an administrator can place a client in travel mode to prevent it from being installed in sites unnecessarily.

Installing and Configuring Remote Utilities on Client Computers

37. True/False: The Remote Tools Client Agent can only be installed on Windows NT clients.

38. True/False: Only members of Domain Admins can remote control clients.

39. True/False: When multisite clients have conflicting remote control permission settings, the most restrictive set takes precedence.

40. The three levels of remote control access are _____, _____, and _____.

41. True/False: A visible indicator is always displayed to alert clients that a remote session is active.

42. True/False: The slower the processor the more important it is to use a high compression ratio during remote control.

43. When NetBEUI is the only protocol in use at a client, the Remote Tools Client Agent must be configured to bind to _____.

44. Remote diagnostic utilities are available for both _____ and _____ systems.

45. True/False: The remote NT diagnostics program can be used to modify settings such as interrupts and environment variable values.

46. True/False: The Ping Test provided with Remote Tools does not require TCP/IP.

47. A program can be launched remotely on a client using the _____ tool.

Installing and Configuring Windows NT Event to SNMP Trap Translator

48. The Event to Trap Translator generates _____ trap messages.

49. The Event to Trap Translator requires that NT clients have both the _____ protocol and the _____ agent installed.

50. The default SNMP community name _____?

Installing and Configuring Health Monitor to Monitor Windows NT Server Computers

51. When monitoring physical disk status you must first enable disk performance counters by running _____.

52. True/False: The Health Monitor Agent can be installed on any SMS 2 site system.

4-1 Which of the following logon scripts are modified upon selecting the option Modify Login Scripts for NetWare 3.*x* clients?

    A. System Login script

    B. All User Login scripts

    C. Specified Container Login scripts

    D. The Default Login script

4-2 After enabling Network Discovery and setting the SNMP configuration options, the administrator notices that only resources on the site servers subnet are being discovered.

Which of the following steps should the administrator perform in order to collect information from the additional subnets?

    A. Update the schedule.

    B. Run Network Trace to determine the topology.

    C. Increase the Hop Count.

    D. Enable Heartbeat Discovery.

4-3 The administrator wants to ensure that all site servers are discovered as resources. Which of the following resource discovery methods must the administrator enable?

    A. Heartbeat Discovery

    B. Network Discovery

    C. Windows NT Networking Logon Discovery

    D. None of the above

4-4 Which of the following protocols can be bound to the Remote Tools Client Agent?

    A. NetBEUI

    B. TCP/IP

C. DLC

D. AppleTalk

E. IPX

4-5   The administrator has discovered approximately 200 potential client resources on a given subnet. The administrator wants to initiate the installation of SMS client software based upon NT group memberships.

Which of the following methodologies should the administrator follow to control the installation of SMS client software on a per-group basis?

A. Reconfigure the network topology so that only one group is represented per subnet.

B. Enable NetWare NDS Server Logon Client Installation and place groups in separate containers.

C. Contact all members of the selected groups using an e-mail message. Include in the e-mail message a link from which to execute either `sms.exe` or `smsman16.exe`.

D. Enable Windows Networking Logon Client Installation; deselect the option to Modify User Logon Scripts; modify the profile of members of the selected groups to call `smsls.bat`.

4-6   Which of the following discovery methods should the administrator enable to periodically reverify resources such as an SQL server?

A. Windows NT Remote Client Discovery

B. Windows Networking Logon Discovery

C. Network Discovery

D. Heartbeat Discovery

4-7   When a client is discovered through the use of Windows Networking Logon Discovery, to where does it copy its Discovery Data Record?

A. To a client access point

B. To the SQL server

C. To the site server

D. To the NETLOGON share

4-8   Which of the following statements are true about the Remote Tools Client Agent?

    A. It can run only on Windows NT clients.

    B. The most restrictive set of permissions applies for multisite clients.

    C. Only members of Domain Admins can remote control NT clients.

    D. Multiple protocols can be bound to it simultaneously.

4-9   Which of the following steps must the administrator perform to generate trap messages if the SQL server records unauthorized logon attempts in the Application Log?

    A. Install the SNMP agent on the SQL server.

    B. Install TCP/IP on the SQL server.

    C. Enter the Event Source and Event ID used to identify unauthorized logon attempts to the SQL server.

    D. Configure the SNMP agent to forward traps to a third-party SNMP manager.

4-10   Which of the following statements about resource discovery is true?

    A. A single resource can exist in only a single SMS site.

    B. Only resources in defined sites can be discovered.

    C. Only resources with an IP address can be discovered.

    D. Resource discovery can include routers and printers.

U N I T

5

Monitoring
and Optimization

Test Objectives

- **Identify changes to a site server after SMS installation. Types of site servers are domain controllers, nondomain controllers, and secondary site servers.**

- **Monitor SMS status messages.**
  - Configure status messages.
  - Configure and use SMS Status Message Viewer.
  - Configure and use SMS logs to monitor SMS process activity.

- **Monitor the progress of SMS functions.**
  - Monitor the progress of client installation.
  - Monitor the progress of inventory collection.
  - Monitor the progress of software distribution.
  - Monitor the progress of remote control.
  - Monitor the progress of software metering.

- **Use SMS utilities to monitor SMS functions.**
  - Use the Windows NT Event Viewer to view SMS error messages.
  - Use the Status Message Viewer to monitor SMS components and processes.
  - Use Network Monitor to view and filter network traffic.
  - Use Network Trace to trace the SMS network.
  - Use SMS Trace to track and view log files.

- **Optimize SQL Server for SMS.**

- **Optimize sender network utilization.**

- **Monitor the SMS database.**
  - Configure SMS database maintenance tasks.
  - Back up and restore the site database.

- **Back up an SMS site.**

Exam objectives are subject to change at any time without prior notice and at Microsoft's sole discretion. Please visit Microsoft's Training and Certification Web site (www.microsoft.com/Train_Cert/) for the most current listing of exam objectives.

This unit focuses on the key steps you must take in order to monitor and optimize an SMS installation. Areas that will be reviewed include the monitoring of major SMS functions and the use of SMS utilities to monitor both general network traffic and traffic specific to SMS. This unit will also take a closer look at how SMS interacts with Microsoft SQL Server and how to maintain the SMS database.

Identifying Changes to a Site Server after SMS Installation

This section will review the modifications SMS makes to the various site servers. A proper understanding of the changes made to site servers is critical to the monitoring, optimization, and troubleshooting processes.

SMS relies on the NT registry as a repository for component and agent parameters. Although you'll probably only rarely modify registry information, you'll frequently need to review registry settings to confirm proper installation and configuration or to identify the relationship between components and files.

Because the exam objective focuses on registry changes made to site servers, you will want to know which hives are affected by SMS. You won't need to memorize each of the various keys and values associated with the SMS components, but you should be aware of where changes are held in the registry.

The next sections summarize the various registry keys and their functions as they relate to SMS.

HKEY_LOCAL_MACHINE\SOFTWARE\Microsoft\SMS

This key holds most of the SMS parameters. The specific details handled by each of the subkeys is perhaps beyond the scope of the exam, but a brief summary of each is provided here:

AdminUI   Provides language and connection information used by the SMS Administrator Console

Client   Provides configuration information for each of the client components installed on the system, paths to client directories, and a listing of sites in which the client is installed

Components   Provides configuration for each of the site system components installed on the system

Compression   Provides compression settings, including the name of the DLL used to compress packages before directing them to child sites

Identification   Provides general SMS identification, including domain name, server name, parent site code, site name, and so forth

Inbox Source   Provides a correlation of names between inboxes and their associated physical directories

Profiles In Use   Provides security ID (SID) info. For example, S-1-5-21-482952865-1621720398-378935785-1012.

Providers   Provides the name of the SQL server and database associated with given sites

Remote Control Temp   Provides the coordinates used to display the visible indicator during remote control sessions

Setup   Provides product registration information and the name of the installation directory

SQL Server   Provides details of how SQL Server is used by the site, including the database name, device names, and paths

Tracing   Provides the name and maximum size of the log file corresponding with each of the SMS components

Triggers   Provides information on the insert, update, and delete triggers SMS places on selected SQL tables

HKEY_LOCAL_MACHINE\SYSTEM\CurrentControlSet\ Services

SMS inserts subkeys at this location for each of the various SMS services installed on the system. Keep in mind that many SMS components run as threads of the SMS_EXECUTIVE service, so there are actually very few entries. Each entry includes startup information for a given service. The services receiving entries under this key on IRONMAN include:

- SMS_EXECUTIVE
- SMS_NT_LOGON_DISCOVERY_AGENT
- SMS_SITE_COMPONENT_MANAGER
- SMS_SQL_MONITOR
- SMSPerfCounters
- Crystal Info Agent
- Crystal Info APS
- Crystal Info Sentinel

HKEY_LOCAL_MACHINE\SOFTWARE\Microsoft\NAL

The NAL subkey holds information related to the Network Abstraction Layer (NAL). A computer system attempting to make contact with site systems across the network checks the NAL to determine the proper provider to use. Examples of provider entries include LOCAL, MSWNET, NWBIND, and NWNDS. SMS includes remote control tools in the Microsoft Resource Kit 4.5 to adjust these settings on the client from the command line prompt.

Share points provide both SMS clients and site with access to the directories used to hold SMS files. The system roles that a server performs dictate which shares and directories will be created. The shares and directories that are active on IRONMAN are listed here.

Share	Directory	Description
CAP_TPA	E:\CAP_TPA	Client Access Point
Cinfo	E:\SMS\Cinfo	Crystal Info

Share	Directory	Description
LicMtr	`C:\SWMTR`	Software Metering
NETLOGON	`C:\WINNT\SYSTEM32\REPL\IMPORT\SCRIPTS`	Logon Point
SMS_SITE	`E:\SMS\inboxes\despoolr.box\receive`	Receiver Inboxes
SMS_TPA	`E:\SMS`	SMS Site Root
SMS_LOGON	`E:\SMSLOGON`	SMS Logon Service
SMSPKGE$	`E:\SMSPKGE$`	Package Directory

Security is maintained by controlling access to share points and by implementing Windows NT file system (NTFS) security. Although users and guests are both granted Change permissions to client access points (CAPs) of NT site systems, NTFS permissions enforce more stringent control in various subdirectories. For example, the users group has Change permissions in the `ccr.box` directory but is restricted to Read permissions in the `clicomp.box`.

The SMS services are responsible for all communication and processing performed by site servers. They are in essence the active components of SMS. The active SMS services on IRONMAN are listed here:

- Info Agent
- Info APS
- Info Sentinel
- SMS Client Service
- SMS_EXECUTIVE
- SMS_LICENSE_SERVER
- SMS_SITE_COMPONENT_MANAGER
- SMS_SQL_MONITOR
- Windows Management

The services can be controlled from Control Panel, Server Manager, or the command prompt using the Net Start command.

Because many of the services are multithreaded, the provision to control the state of individual threads was required. To start, stop, and configure logging for individual threads, use the SMS Service Manager.

Errors related to the starting and operation of the services, if any, will be recorded in the NT Event Log.

Monitoring SMS Status Messages

SMS provides reporting and logging functions that you can use to monitor continually both the state of individual components and the overall health of sites. This section reviews status reporting configuration and the way various SMS logs correlate to specific functions.

Configuring Status Messages

The overall site status is summarized to make it quickly discernible if any individual components are malfunctioning. The status of each component, service, and thread is determined individually by comparing the number of error, warning, and informational messages against assigned thresholds.

Although it is unlikely that you will need to modify the default settings, you should be aware of the steps involved if it's ever required. Changes can affect status reporting in three areas in the SMS Administrator Console. Each of these areas of configuration is described here.

Status Reporting

Status Reporting settings (see Figure 5.1) control the overall reporting properties for both server and client components. You can specify the level of detail that you want reported by the components, and you can elect to report status messages to the status server, NT Event Log, or both.

You should consider the ramifications of adjusting the level of reporting from the default settings. As with any auditing function, you need to establish a proper balance between the level of detail required for accuracy and the amount of system resources that can be allocated to the task.

Status Summarizer

The Status Summarizer determines the overall status of site systems, components, advertisements, and packages by reviewing the number of status messages generated for components versus threshold levels.

You can control the Status Summarizer settings for site systems, advertisements, and components, as described in the following section; however, you cannot modify the package summarization properties.

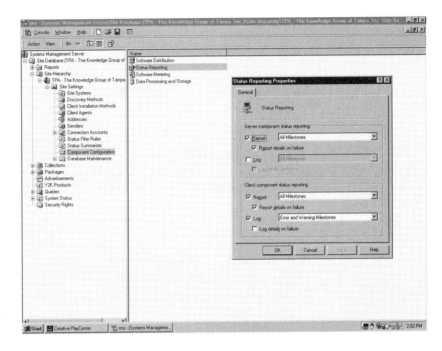

Site System Status Summarizer   This summarizer determines the overall status of the site systems. The status messages generated for the site system roles are periodically evaluated against the thresholds set here, to determine current status.

The properties window contains two settings tabs, as shown in Figure 5.2.

The General tab is used to enable or disable the summarization of related status messages, specify the summarization schedule, and determine whether site system status will be replicated to a parent site.

The Threshold tab allows you to modify the assigned warning and critical thresholds for storage objects used by the site systems (e.g., the SQL database and transaction log).

Component Status Summarizer   This summarizer determines the overall status of individual services and threads such as the SMS_EXECUTIVE and SMS_INBOX_MANAGER. The settings in the properties window are similar to those of the Site System Status Summarizer, except the thresholds are based on the number of messages of a specific type being used to determine the site status level as OK, Warning, or Critical.

Advertisement Status Summarizer   This summarizer determines the status of advertisements based on success or failure of the receipt of advertisements or execution of associated programs. You do not establish thresholds for this summarizer; you only control whether it is enabled and whether it should report information to a parent site.

FIGURE 5.2

The General properties tab of the Site System Status Summarizer

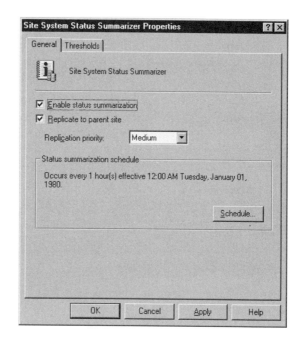

Status Filter Rules

You can implement status filter rules in order to have the Status Manager handle the reporting of individual status messages differently, depending on actions you define. For example, if a message were to arrive from a particular component or with a certain severity you may want to include it in the NT Event Log or prevent it from being included into the summarized status.

Configuring and Using SMS Status Message Viewer

Status messages can be displayed using the SMS Status Message Viewer. You can specify all messages to be displayed or you can choose to display only informational, warning, or error messages.

Configuring and Using SMS Logs to Monitor SMS Process Activity

Each of the SMS services and threads can report information to assigned logs. This section focuses on correlating the services and logs; Unit 6 will delve deeper into how to monitor and read the logs using SMS Trace and TRACER.

You can modify the log settings located in the registry subkey HKEY_LOCAL_MACHINE\SOFTWARE\Microsoft\SMS\Tracing, by using regedt32.exe.

It is highly unlikely that you will be asked on the exam which log corresponds with a particular service. However, a table correlating services and their logs is provided here as a reference.

Don't try to memorize the table that follows. It is simply provided as a reference to be used in following sections.

Component	Log
LICENSE_METERING	licsrvc.log
SMS_CLIENT_CONFIG_MANAGER	ccm.log
SMS_CLIENT_INSTALL_DATA_MGR	cidm.log
SMS_COLLECTION_EVALUATOR	colleval.log
SMS_COMPONENT_STATUS_SUMMARIZER	compsumm.log
SMS_COURIER_SENDER_CONFIRMATION	cscnfsvc.log
SMS_DESPOOLER	despool.log
SMS_DISCOVERY_DATA_MANAGER	ddm.log
SMS_DISTRIBUTION_MANAGER	distmgr.log
SMS_EXECUTIVE	smsexec.log
SMS_HIERARCHY_MANAGER	hman.log

Component	Log
SMS_INBOX_MANAGER	inboxmgr.log
SMS_INBOX_MANAGER_ASSISTANT	inboxast.log
SMS_INVENTORY_DATA_LOADER	dataldr.log
SMS_INVENTORY_PROCESSOR	invproc.log
SMS_LAN_SENDER	sender.log
SMS_LICENSE_SERVER_MANAGER	licsvcfg.log
SMS_MAC_PATH_MANAGER	macpath.log
SMS_NDS_LOGON_DISCOVERY_MANAGER	ndlgdscm.log
SMS_NDS_LOGON_INSTALLATION_MANAGER	ndlginst.log
SMS_NDS_LOGON_MANAGER	nd_logon.log
SMS_NETWORK_DISCOVERY	netdisc.log
SMS_NT_LOGON_DISCOVERY_AGENT	ntlgdsca.log
SMS_NT_LOGON_DISCOVERY_MANAGER	ntlgdscm.log
SMS_NT_LOGON_INSTALLATION_MANAGER	ntlginst.log
SMS_NT_LOGON_MANAGER	nt_logon.log
SMS_NT_USER_DISCOVERY_AGENT	ntusrdis.log
SMS_NT_USER_GROUP_DISCOVERY_AGENT	ntug_dis.log
SMS_NW_LOGON_DISCOVERY_MANAGER	nwlgdscm.log
SMS_NW_LOGON_INSTALLATION_MANAGER	nwlginst.log
SMS_NW_LOGON_MANAGER	nw_logon.log
SMS_NWBIND_SERVER_DISCOVERY_AGENT	offersum.log

Component	Log
SMS_REPLICATION_MANAGER	replmgr.log
SMS_SCHEDULER	sched.log
SMS_SITE_COMPONENT_MANAGER	sitecomp.log
SMS_SITE_CONTROL_MANAGER	sitectrl.log
SMS_SITE_SYSTEM_STATUS_SUMMARIZER	sitestat.log
SMS_SOFTWARE_INVENTORY_PROCESSOR	sinvproc.log
SMS_SQL_MONITOR	smsdbmon.log
SMS_STATUS_MANAGER	nwsrvdis.log
SMS_OFFER_MANAGER	offermgr.log
SMS_OFFER_STATUS_SUMMARIZER	statmgr.log
SMS_USER_INTERFACE	ui.log
SMS_WINNT_REMOTE_CLIENT_INSTALL_MANAGER	nt_push.log
SMS_WINNT_SERVER_DISCOVERY_AGENT	ntsrvdis.log

For each of the services and threads you can control whether logging is enabled and, if it is, the maximum size of the log file and the name of the log file. I would highly recommend not modifying the names of the log files so they remain consistent with other documentation; however, you may find it necessary to reduce or increase the maximum log file sizes. The default log sizes are 1MB for each server log and 100K for each client log.

In addition to the list of server-side logs listed here, there are several log files housed on SMS clients that are helpful for troubleshooting hardware inventory (hinv32.log), software inventory (sinv32.log), software metering (liccli.log), and communication with CAPs by the SMS Copy Queue Manager (cqmgr32.log).

Monitoring the Progress of SMS Processes

Much of the information in the previous section pertained to the correlation of services and threads with log files on the site server. This section will focus on the manner in which data flows between 32-bit SMS client systems and the site server, and how the flow can be monitored using log files. The areas defined herein pertain to inventory collection, software distribution, remote control, and software metering.

Monitoring the Progress of Client Installation

The installation and update of client-side components are primarily the responsibilities of the Client Component Installation Manager (CCIM). Log files for the client agents are located in the client's `\%WINDIR%\MS\SMS\LOGS` directory and can be viewed with any text editor or by using SMS Trace or TRACER.

Monitoring the Progress of Inventory Collection

The monitoring of inventory collection involves being familiar with the processes used when collecting either hardware or software inventory. The following sections list the primary components involved in each collection method and the necessary server and client-side log files to monitor.

Monitoring 32-Bit Client Hardware Inventory

The following list outlines the hardware inventory process from the installation of the client agent to the recording in the site database:

1. The Hardware Inventory Agent is installed (`inhinv32.log`).

2. The Hardware Inventory Agent is run according to the schedule set at the site from which the client installed the agent (`hinv32.log`). The inventory frequency can be found under `HKLM\SW\MS\SMS\Client\ Sites\<SiteCode>\Client Components\Hardware Inventory Agent`.

An initial hardware inventory is performed 15 minutes after the agent is first installed. Because this is not linked to logon, it is less intrusive than the hardware collection process in previous versions.

3. The agent queries the CIM object manager for the data corresponding to the enabled classes and properties in the sms_def.mof. This information is then used to create either a complete hardware inventory record (*.hic) or a record of changes (*.hid).

4. The Copy Queue Manager copies the inventory file to the inventry.box file on the client's CAP with a unique name and new extension (cqmgr32.dll).

5. Either the Inbox Manager Assistant (inboxast.log)or the Inbox Manager moves the inventory file to the Inventory Processor inbox.

The Inbox Manager running on the site server performs the periodic polling of NetWare-based CAPs. For this reason the site server must have either Gateway Services for NetWare (GSNW) or the IntraNetWare client installed when using NetWare-based site systems.

6. The Inventory Processor determines if the file received contains complete or delta information (invproc.log). The record is then forwarded with a new header to the Inventory Data Loader.

7. The Inventory Data Loader records the information in the database (dataldr.log).

Monitoring 32-Bit Client Software Inventory

The following list provide an overview of the software inventory process:

1. The Software Inventory Agent is installed (insinv32.log; also ccim32.log, clisvc.log).

2. The Software Inventory Agent is run according to the schedule set at the site from which the client installed the agent (sinv32.log).

NOTE   The initial software inventory is performed 30 minutes after the agent is installed.

3. The Software Inventory Agent creates an inventory file with an extension of either .sic or .sid, depending on whether the file contains a complete or delta software inventory.

4. The Copy Queue Manager copies the inventory file to the sinv.box on the client's CAP (cqmgr32.log).

5. Either the Inbox Manager Assistant (inboxast.log) or the Inbox Manager moves the inventory file to the Software Inventory Processor inbox.

6. The Software Inventory Processor then records the information in the site database (sinvproc.log).

Monitoring the Progress of Software Distribution

The two aspects of software distribution that you will need to monitor are package distribution and advertisement. Because the details of the distribution process have been discussed in earlier units, this section will limit the details to the aspects that require monitoring only.

The Distribution Manager has the primary responsibility in the creation and distribution of packages (distmgr.log). Additionally, the sender (sender.log) will come into play if a package is being sent to a distribution point in a child site.

The status of the distribution process can be viewed for individual packages under the Distribution Status key in the Administrator Console. The status of the distribution process to each distribution point is recorded.

The notification to clients that a package is available for installation is primarily the responsibility of the Available Programs Monitor (smsapm32 .log) and the Offer Manager (offermgr.log). The Offer Manager has the duty of keeping the lookup (.lkp) files on CAPs updated. The lookup files are used to identify which clients should receive a given advertisement.

By viewing the summarized advertisement status data and the associated status messages, you can determine which advertisements have been received and executed successfully or unsuccessfully. More detailed information can be seen on a per client basis by viewing the client's related log files, including `smsapm32.log`, `odpsys32.log`, `odpusr32.log`, and `odpwnt32.log`.

Monitoring the Progress of Remote Control

Although the remote control agent does not maintain log files, you can review status messages generated by clients to determine who has attempted to remotely control a client. The status message provides details of which client was accessed, from which system, and when the access occurred.

In addition to the status messages, the NT security log also records information related to remote sessions. Keep in mind that although the Permitted Viewers list on the client ultimately determines access, rights can also be controlled by setting instance rights to collections.

You can execute the `remote.exe` utility in order to remote control clients without requiring that you run the SMS Administrator Console.

Monitoring the Progress of Software Metering

The client's `liccli.log` file details all of the software metering agent's communication with metering servers. By viewing the log file, you can determine the client configuration, which programs the agent will ignore (excluded applications), and the requesting and granting of licenses.

Using SMS Utilities to Monitor SMS Functions

S MS includes many utilities that can be used to track the performance and status of the SMS processes. This section will review the basic functions of the Windows NT Event Viewer, Status Message Viewer, Network Monitor, and Network Trace. The intention is not to provide an all-inclusive summary of the utilities' details, but rather to review the times when the use of a particular utility is appropriate.

SMS processes should be monitored as part of the normal maintenance routine. Identifying potential problems early allows for a proactive approach to issues that may arise.

Using the Windows NT Event Viewer to View SMS Error Messages

As mentioned earlier, status filter rules can be created to specify which status messages should be recorded in the Windows NT Event Log. In addition to recorded status messages, the event log will reflect any issues related to the startup and operation of SMS services and components.

The events will be recorded to the application log, with the exception of issues that involve security, such as remote control, which are recorded in the security log.

Using the Status Message Viewer to Monitor SMS Components and Processes

After being alerted to potential issues by the Status Summarizer, you will no doubt want to get more detailed information on what may have caused a warning or critical status. The details of status messages are easily obtained using the Status Message Viewer.

Using Network Monitor to View and Filter Network Traffic

The Network Monitor is a software-based protocol analyzer that allows you to monitor, capture, and decipher network traffic. Unlike the version of Network Monitor that comes as part of Windows NT, this version uses a promiscuous driver, allowing it to capture all network traffic on a segment, regardless of destination.

In order to assist in the analysis of captured traffic, Network Monitor includes a series of experts that can be used to interpret the data. The experts can report such information as Average Server Response Time, Top Users, and Protocol Distribution.

As an extension to Network Monitor the Network Monitor Control can be configured and run in order to monitor network segments for certain conditions, including the presence of rogue DHCP or Windows Internet Naming

Service (WINS) servers, invalid IP addresses, invalid IPX addresses, SYN attacks, and the use of monitoring tools.

A primary advantage of using the Network Monitor Control Tool over simply analyzing captured data is that it reports conditions based on real-time data collection. Although it does not take specific actions when a condition is identified, it is still a powerful tool.

Using Network Trace to Trace the SMS Network

The primary purpose of Network Trace is to provide a clear picture of the relationships among SMS site systems and to identify the roles of each. Additionally, by selectively pinging one or all of the site systems displayed you can confirm the connectivity between site systems.

The information detailing the routes connecting the SMS site systems is determined by using the tracert command.

Using SMS Trace to Track and View Log Files

SMS Trace allows you to view multiple server and client log files in real-time. The SMS Trace utility is not installed as part of the server or client installation but is included with the SMS CD-ROM.

To install SMS Trace on an Intel-based system run traceinst.exe from the SMS CD-ROM's \Support\Reskit\Bin\i386\Smstrace folder. The utility for Alpha-based systems can be found in \Support\Reskit\Bin\Alpha\ Smstrace.

SMS Trace is perhaps the most effective means of determining where a breakdown occurs in any SMS procedure. For example, assume that a client was not properly reporting hardware inventory. You could use SMS trace to view the client's log files simultaneously to confirm that the Hardware Inventory Agent processes inventory data on the client (hinv32.log) and then that the data are successfully passed to a client access point by the Copy Queue Manager (cqmgr32.log).

By using SMS Trace, you can determine that in the case of the example shown in Figure 5.3 the inventory agent is performing properly; however, the Copy Queue Manager is having difficulty communicating with the designated CAP.

FIGURE 5.3

Viewing multiple log files using SMS Trace

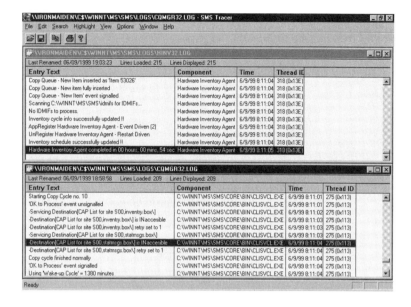

Optimizing SQL Server for SMS

Optimizing SQL Server will be simpler if you use version 7 instead of version 6.5. This is because many of the optimization tasks that you need to perform in version 6.5 are automated in version 7. Regardless of the version, however, there are several basic concepts that you need to know. The following list details some basic optimization concepts for SQL Server that are common to both versions:

Separate SMS data and logs on separate physical disks   In version 6.5 this requires creating separate devices on the disks before installing SMS. When using version 7, simply specify separate drives when creating the data (.mdf) and log (.ldf) files during SMS setup.

Ensure sufficient space in tempdb   The tempdb database file is used in both versions as workspace during Order by and Group by operations, and for storing temporary tables and server-side cursors. Tempdb should be set to approximately 20 percent of the SMS data size. For example, queries against an SMS database containing 500MB of data would benefit from a tempdb of 100MB.

Additional information regarding the installation and tuning of SQL Server is provided in Unit 1.

Optimizing Sender Network Utilization

To optimize sender network traffic, first you must have a good handle on the amount of data transferred between sites, the frequency with which the transfer is performed, and both the available and the potential bandwidths between sites. The best time to determine bandwidth utilization and the impact the SMS will have on its availability is before installing SMS.

If you have implemented the proper number and types of senders based on information provided earlier, there is little that should be required at this point to optimize sender utilization. The primary configurable setting is the number of maximum concurrent sendings allowed in total and per site. Increasing either of these settings will increase a sender's capacity to transfer data between sites. Remember, though, that the additional data transfer is at the expense of network bandwidth availability.

Monitoring the SMS Database

The SMS database can be monitored in order to ensure that enough SQL resources are available, including space in the SMS database and transaction log. SQL Server provides performance monitor objects that can be used to determine if any action is required.

Configuring SMS Database Maintenance Tasks

The SMS database maintenance tasks simplify the upkeep of the SMS database by automating tasks. The following list summarizes the various tasks:

Export Site Database   Disabled by default, this task exports a copy of the site database to a SQL dump device.

Export Site Database Transaction Log   Disabled by default, this task exports a copy of the site database transaction log to a SQL dump device.

Export Software Metering Database   Disabled by default, this task exports a copy of the software metering database to a SQL dump device.

Export Software Metering Database Transaction Log   Disabled by default, this task exports a copy of the software metering database transaction log to a SQL dump device.

Backup SMS Site Server   Disabled by default, this task backs up the SQL databases, registry keys, and SMS directories to a directory you specify.

Update Statistics   Enabled by default (M, W, F, Sat), this task updates the information used by the SQL query optimizer.

Rebuild Indexes   Enabled by default (Sun), this task is used to reorganize the indexes and reduce fragmentation.

Monitor Keys and Re-create Views   Enabled by default (Sun), this task generates a status message if a problem is detected with the relational integrity between tables. This task also re-creates views if necessary.

Delete Aged Inventory History   Enabled by default (90 days), this task removes inventory data more than 90 days old.

Delete Aged Status Messages   Enabled by default (once per day), this task removes status messages based on status filter rules.

Delete Aged Collected Files   Enabled by default (90 days), this task removes collected files more than 90 days old.

Delete Aged Discovery Data   Enabled by default (90 days), this task removes Discovery Data Records more than 90 days old.

Backing Up and Restoring the Site Database

Backing up the site database is fairly simple; it can be automated using either the export site database task or SQL Enterprise manager. The backup is usually directed onto a tape device but can also be directed to disk.

Restoring the site database is also simple, as long as you follow a few basic steps:

1. Stop all SMS-related services, so the database is not in use.

2. Restore the SMS database. SQL Server must use the same processor type, sort order, and character set as the original.

3. Run SMS Setup on the site server, and update the name of the SQL server and any SQL names that have changed.

4. Restart the SMS services.

Backing Up an SMS Site

Backing up the SMS site involves more than just backing up the SMS database. Besides backing up the SMS database as outlined earlier, you have to back up the SMS directory (the `sitectrl.ct0` file at a minimum), and registry keys (SMS and NAL).

When restoring the SMS site server, the system must have certain characteristics identical to the original, including computer name, domain name, processor type, and installation directory.

If a registry key fails to restore, you may not have sufficient permissions or the key may be in use (even after stopping all SMS services). You can usually resolve this by setting all SMS services to manual, and then rebooting. After restoring is completed, you must set the services back to automatic and reboot.

STUDY QUESTIONS

Identifying Changes to a Site Server after SMS Installation

1. The _____ registry key holds most of the SMS configuration parameters.

2. The _____ registry key holds the startup information for the SMS Executive.

3. The volume used for a CAP must have the _____ file system.

4. To start an individual thread, you should use the SMS _____ _____.

Monitoring SMS Status Messages

5. Errors starting the services will be recorded in the _____.

6. The status of system components is determined by comparing the number of messages of various types against _____.

7. Overall status reporting properties are controlled via the _____ section of the SMS Administrator Console.

8. True/False: You can control the Status Summarizer settings for package summarization.

9. True/False: Status messages are always reported to parent sites.

10. The three status message levels are: _____, _____, and _____.

11. If you want a particular message to be recorded in the NT Event Log, you should define it in the _____.

12. True/False: By default, logging is enabled for all threads.

13. The default maximum log size for client logs is _____ .

14. The default maximum log size for server logs is _____.

15. The installation log file for the Hardware Inventory Agent is _____.

16. The software metering log file on the client is _____.

17. Communication between clients and CAPs is recorded in the client's _____ file.

Monitoring the Progress of SMS Processes

18. The _____ is primarily responsible for installation of client agents.

19. True/False: SMS logs can be viewed with any text editor.

20. Initial hardware inventory collection is performed _____ minutes after the agent is first installed.

21. The running of the Hardware Inventory Agent is recorded in the _____ file.

22. The base file for determining which hardware classes and properties to report is the _____ file.

23. A hardware inventory file with an extension of _____ signifies it is a complete inventory.

24. A hardware inventory file with an extension of _____ signifies it is a partial inventory.

25. The _____ Manager is responsible for polling NetWare-based CAPs.

26. To connect to NetWare CAPs, the site server requires either _____ or _____ to be installed.

27. The installation of the Software Inventory Agent is recorded in the _____ file.

28. The initial software inventory is performed _____ minutes after the agent is installed.

29. A software inventory file with an extension of _____ signifies that it is a complete inventory.

30. Creation and distribution of packages is primarily the responsibility of the _____.

31. When packages are sent between sites, the transmission of the data is recorded in the _____ file.

32. True/False: The remote control agent does not have a log file.

33. Access to clients via remote control is recorded in the NT _____ log.

34. Only persons or groups in the _____ list can remote control a client.

35. The primary client log for software metering is the _____ file.

36. Programs can be _____ to prevent them from being metered.

37. Most SMS service errors are recorded in the NT _____ log.

38. Details of SMS messages can be viewed using the _____ _____ viewer.

Using SMS Utilities to Monitor SMS Functions

39. The Network Monitor uses a _____ driver.

S T U D Y   Q U E S T I O N S

40. Data captured using Network Monitor can be deciphered easily using

_____.

41. Name three items that the Network Monitor Experts can determine.

42. The presence of rogue DHCP servers or invalid IP addresses can be determined using the

_____ _____ _____ _____.

43. True/False: The Network Monitor Control Tool can take action based on its findings.

44. _____ provides a graphical view of the relationship

between SMS site systems.

45. The _____command is used to determine the route between systems.

Optimizing SQL Server for SMS

46. True/False: It is best to store the SMS data and SMS log on the same physical device.

47. Increasing the size of the _____ database can aid in certain queries.

Optimizing Sender Network Utilization

48. True/False: Increasing the maximum concurrent sendings per site is done at the expense of available bandwidth.

Monitoring the SMS Database

49. Exporting the site database copies the database to a _____ device.

50. By default, the Aged Discovery task removes data older than _____ days.

51. The _____ task is run four times a week to provide updated information for the SQL query optimizer.

Backing Up an SMS Site

52. True/False: When backing up the SMS database, you must first stop SQL Server.

53. True/False: SMS Setup can be used to physically move the SQL database to a new server.

54. When backing up the SMS Site Server, you should back up the database, the SMS directory, and the _____.

S A M P L E   T E S T

5-1 What is the most effective way of limiting the amount of status message data transferred to parent sites, without stopping the flow of status messages completely?

  A. Change the priority of status messages to low.

  B. Create Status Filter Rules.

  C. Stop unnecessary services.

  D. Forward status messages to the Status Summarizer.

5-2 Example Company's administrator is having problems with Network Discovery. When he tries to view the `netdisc.log` file, it cannot be found.

  What is the probable reason that the log file does not exist?

  A. Logging for Network Discovery was not enabled.

  B. Problems with Network Discovery prevented the log from being created.

  C. The log exceeded its maximum allowed size and was deleted.

  D. The log file was renamed.

5-3 Which utility provides a means of viewing multiple SMS logs simultaneously while they are being updated?

  A. TRACER

  B. SMS Trace

  C. SMS Administrator Console

  D. MOF Manager

5-4 The SMS administrator for Example Company selected support for Novell NetWare Bindery Servers during installation. However, while attempting to create CAPs on a NetWare 3.12 server, he is encountering errors when trying to connect to the NetWare server.

Which of the following are possible causes for the errors?

    A. The IntraNetWare client is not installed on the site server.

    B. GSNW is not installed on the site server.

    C. NWLink, the IPX/SPX-compatible transport, is not installed on the site server.

    D. NetWare 3.12 servers cannot be CAPs.

5-5 The administrator has disabled the hardware and software inventory agents at the central site; however, even after a week, certain clients continue to report information.

What is the most likely reason for this?

    A. The clients have not realized the agents should be removed.

    B. The clients are not logging on the domain.

    C. The clients have not rebooted.

    D. The clients are members of multiple sites.

5-6 Although Allen is a member of the SMS Admins group, he is being denied access when attempting to remote control any of his site's members.

What is the most likely reason for this?

    A. The SMS Admins group is not in the Permitted Viewers list.

    B. The link to the client systems is less than 56kbps.

    C. The clients have the wrong protocol bound.

    D. Allen is not logged on to the domain.

5-7 The administrator is concerned that users in test labs are installing DHCP servers and affecting corporate users' IP assignments.

Which of the following utilities should the administrator use to monitor for the rogue DHCP servers?

A. Network Monitor

B. Performance Monitor

C. Network Monitor Control Tool

D. Network Trace

5-8 Which of the following utilities should the administrator use to identify the relationship between SMS site systems?

A. Network Monitor

B. Performance Monitor

C. Network Monitor Control Tool

D. Network Trace

5-9 The SMS administrator has noticed that certain queries return information very slowly.

Which of the following tasks may increase the speed of the queries?

A. Rebuild indexes.

B. Update statistics.

C. Monitor keys and re-create views.

D. Export site database.

5-10 The SQL administrator wants to have the SMS database moved to a new SQL server. Which of the following items must be configured on the new SQL server as they were on the previous one?

A. Processor type

B. Sort order

C. Character set

D. Security mode

5-11 When backing up an SMS database, the administrator does not get an option to back up the transaction log. What is the probable cause?

A. The transaction log is on a different device than the data.

B. The transaction log is on the same device as the data.

C. The tempdb database is full.

D. The database option Truncate Logon Checkpoint is on.

UNIT

6

Troubleshooting

Test Objectives

- **Choose the appropriate diagnostic tool.**

- **Diagnose and resolve installation problems in SMS site systems.**
  - Diagnose and resolve installation problems involving the primary site server.
  - Diagnose and resolve installation problems involving the secondary site server.
  - Diagnose and resolve installation problems involving client access points, distribution points, and component servers.

- **Diagnose and resolve installation problems involving client computers.**

- **Diagnose and resolve problems involving software distribution.**

- **Diagnose and resolve problems involving inventory collection.**

- **Diagnose and resolve problems involving remote control.**

- **Diagnose and resolve problems involving software metering.**

- **Diagnose and resolve problems involving SNMP integration.**

- **Restore an SMS site.**
  - Restore a SQL Server.
  - Restore a site server.
  - Restore logon points, client access points, and distribution points.

- **Diagnose and resolve problems involving site-to-site communication.**

Exam objectives are subject to change at any time without prior notice and at Microsoft's sole discretion. Please visit Microsoft's Training and Certification Web site (www.microsoft.com/Train_Cert/) for the most current listing of exam objectives.

This chapter will discuss the diagnosis and resolution of various SMS problems, focusing on the most common problems you'll face in a number of situations. Your own personal troubleshooting methods will not be as important to doing well on the exam as making sure you can determine the cause of basic problems and take appropriate action.

Choosing the Appropriate Diagnostic Tool

The exam will test your knowledge of various diagnostic tools. Given a particular scenario or problem, you will need to identify which diagnostic tool is best suited to the task.

Specific diagnostic tools you will want to be familiar with include:

- Network Monitor: Use this tool to capture and analyze network traffic. Includes network experts that help interpret captured data.

- Network Monitor Control Tool: Use this tool to monitor the network for rogue DHCP or Windows Internet Naming Service (WINS) servers, SYN attacks, invalid IP addresses, unauthorized use of network monitor, and failed routers.

- Dumpsend: Use this tool to extract the contents of send request (.srq) and send status (.srs) files.

- SMS Trace: Use this tool to view both historical and current log entries. Multiple files can be viewed simultaneously.

- WBEMtest: Use this tool to confirm connectivity to the Web-based Enterprise Management (WBEM) repository.

- SMS Status Message Viewer: Use this tool to view details of status messages for SMS components.

This section of the exam will test your ability to identify which diagnostic tool to choose. You'll need to know the purpose of each diagnostic tool, but not the intimate details.

Diagnosing and Resolving SMS Site System Installation Problems

The following sections review symptoms and solutions for many of the common errors encountered during the installation of the primary site server, secondary site server, and site systems. With proper planning, you can avoid most of these problems, but the exam will test your ability to find ready solutions for any problems that do arise.

Diagnosing and Resolving Primary Site Server Installation Problems

If problems occur during the installation of a primary site server, the Setup program usually sends a relatively self-explanatory error message. The most common errors usually involve the Windows NT File System (NTFS) partition, the SMS service account, and the configuration of SQL Server.

If the installation of the primary site server fails, the installation log file, smssetup.log, will remain on the server.

An NTFS partition of at least 1GB must be created before beginning the installation. If an NTFS partition with sufficient free space is not available the Setup program will report the error.

The SMS service account requires membership in the Domain Admins group and the right to log on as a service. If the SMS service account to be used is in a different domain than that of the primary site server or SQL server, then the proper trust relationships must be established.

The successful installation of a primary site server involves the creation of the SMS database on the SQL server. If the SQL server is inaccessible, has insufficient connections, or has devices that are too small, the installation will fail.

The number of SQL user connections should be a minimum of 50, plus 5 for every SMS Administrator Console that will be accessing the database simultaneously.

Diagnosing and Resolving Secondary Site Server Installation Problems

The most common problems encountered during the installation of a secondary site server are caused by improperly preparing the installation partition or the SMS service account. The installation partition must be formatted with NTFS and have at least 500MB of free space. The SMS service account must be created before installation, be granted membership in the Domain Admins group, and be permitted to log on as a service. If you are specifying an SMS service account that resides in another domain, make sure the proper trust relationships exist.

Diagnosing and Resolving Client Access Points, Distribution Points, Logon Points, and Component Servers Installation Problems

The following list details common problems and solutions involving various site system roles:

Clients cannot connect to client access points (CAPs)   Check the client's Cqmgr32.log to confirm its attempt to connect. Verify that the share point has not been removed and that the proper share and NTFS permissions are assigned.

Clients cannot connect to distribution points (DPs)   Make sure that each client's operating system has access to an existing distribution point. This is especially important when you are advertising packages to a collection of clients with mixed operating systems. In addition, confirm share and NTFS permissions.

Clients cannot connect to logon points   Confirm that the proper logon discovery and/or installation methods are enabled.

The site server cannot access component servers   Ensure that the proper connection account exists and that passwords have not been modified.

Diagnosing and Resolving Client Installation Problems

When diagnosing client installation problems, first determine whether the problems are isolated to a single system or whether entire groups of computers are being affected.

If only a single system is experiencing problems that are preventing installation, it is probably because that system has either insufficient disk space or inadequate permissions.

 The minimum available space requirements for an SMS client is 14MB, or 20MB if you choose to enable all optional agents.

When entire groups of computers have installation issues, it is most likely because the proper installation methods are not enabled or the clients are not within the site boundaries.

Diagnosing and Resolving Software Distribution Problems

Software distribution is primarily the responsibility of the Distribution Manager. As the Distribution Manager creates and distributes packages, each of its actions is recorded in the Distmgr.log file. Additionally, status messages are generated when distribution hits key milestones. The details of the status messages can be read using the Status Message Viewer.

When distributing packages, it is important to remember that the site server must be able to connect to all of the distribution points. If NetWare servers are used as distribution points, Gateway Services for NetWare (GSNW) or the IntraNetWare client must be installed.

Diagnosing and Resolving Inventory Collection Problems

Inventory collection can involve hardware, software, and file collection. As with any SMS problem, you must first determine whether it is affecting only a single client or all members of a site.

When all site members are having problems with inventory collection, you need to begin your diagnosis by checking that each of the necessary client agents have been enabled and that a proper schedule has been set.

When dealing with individual client systems that are not reporting inventory properly, check each of the following:

Is the client agent properly installed?   Confirm this by looking at the appropriate agent installation log on the client: either the `Inhinv32.log` (for hardware agents) or the `Insinv32.log` (for software agents).

Is the client a member of multiple sites?   If the client is a member of multiple sites, inventory collection may be working properly, but according to the inventory schedule of its primary site. To make it work according to the client's inventory schedule, you can change the site precedence by using the SMS applet found in control panel.

Does the client have sufficient free disk space?   If the client does not have enough free disk space to generate copies of files you've requested to be collected, the collection will fail. Check `Sinv32.log`, the software inventory agent log file, for possible errors.

Does the client's file size exceed collection limits?   If a file a client is requested to copy to the server exceeds the size limits set for file collection, it will not be reported. In this case, it is possible for a file to be collected from some machines but not others, because of size differences.

Diagnosing and Resolving Remote Control Problems

Problems of being unable to control a client from a remote location usually involve permissions or protocols. The most common remote control problems are listed here:

Is access being denied? Check the Permitted Viewers list on the client to ensure that the proper users and groups are included. If so, check the agent configuration to see if the user needs to confirm remote control permissions. Also, check the NT Security Log for any logon failures.

Is the agent bound to the wrong protocol? The remote control agent can bind only to a single protocol on a client. If the client has multiple protocols, you'll have to confirm that the proper one is linked. The default protocol to bind to is set in the agent configuration for the site; however, it can be overwritten in the client's registry if necessary. Remember that in the Back Office 4.5 Resource Kit you can find command line utilities to change this on the client.

The remote control client agent can bind only to a single protocol. The administrative program will attempt to contact the client using the first eight protocols installed.

Is the client not being found? If a router separates the administrator and the client, you must confirm that the address for the client can be resolved. NetBIOS name resolution can be performed by using a WINS server or manually maintained by using a LMHOSTS file.

Diagnosing and Resolving Software Metering Problems

Software metering can be used both to control license usage and to identify which software packages clients are using. Some of the more common software metering issues follow:

Clients are not being denied access when licenses are exceeded for any products Ensure that the license-metering server is accessible to the clients; otherwise they will work in offline mode. Confirm that the agent is configured to force real-time license verification.

Clients are not being denied access when licenses are exceeded for a specific product   Check that the software is registered as a licensed product. If it is, make sure that the setting to enforce license limits is selected and that the option to wait until a trend has been established to enforce licensing is deselected.

Client agent is not installed   Confirm that the client's operating system is Windows 95/98 or Windows NT 4.*x* or greater.

Clients can circumvent licensing policies by renaming applications   Base the identification of a product on header information, instead of the name as it appears in Explorer. The client would need access to the source code in order to recompile an application with different header information.

Too much space on the site server is being used to maintain licensing information   Change the data summarization times to summarize product usage more frequently. By default, this occurs every 4 hours. Also, it is best to exclude programs for which you do not want to maintain usage statistics.

To view each of the steps a client takes in the license process, you can view the client's `liccli.log` file using SMS Trace.

Diagnosing and Resolving SNMP Integration Problems

SNMP Event to Trap translation is a fairly simple process, because Microsoft provides the agent side. To truly implement this feature, however, you need an SNMP manager such as HP OpenView. Because the use of the agent requires the Windows NT SNMP service, this agent installs only on Windows NT clients.

Common configuration issues related to the SNMP Event to Trap Translator are listed here:

The agent will not install on a client   The agent is supported only on Windows NT clients. Before enabling the agent for the site, you should install the NT SNMP service on the clients.

The agent does not generate any trap messages   This may not seem to be a problem; however, if trap messages should be generated for a particular event, make sure the event is recorded in the Windows NT Event log.

Trap messages are generated but not received   Check the Windows NT SNMP service to confirm the proper trap destination. Also check to make sure you have the same community name on the client that you have on the management console.

Restoring an SMS Site

Restoring SMS site components such as the site server and SQL Server is discussed in Unit 5. The following sections cover specific problems you may encounter during the restoration process.

Restoring a SQL Server

Listed here are problems you may encounter when restoring SMS databases to a SQL server:

The configuration of the new SQL server is different from the original   The new SQL server must have the same processor type, character set, and sort order as the original.

The site server cannot connect to the new SQL server   Make sure that the proper permissions and trusts are in place to enable the SMS service account to access the SQL server. Also, be sure to reset the SMS site to update the registry and point to the new SQL Server.

Restoring a Site Server

Problems specific to the restoration of a site server include:

New equipment is different from original   A site server can only be restored to a system with the same process type, domain name, machine name, and installation drive as the original.

The `sitectrl.ct0` file was not restored   If a copy of the site control file was not made, the site settings will not be accurate. A new copy can be generated by running `preinst.exe /dump`.

Services do not initialize   Ensure that the registry keys (including the SMS and NAL subkeys) were properly restored.

Restoring Logon Points, Client Access Points, and Distribution Points

If a site system playing a supporting role as a logon point, CAP, or DP fails, the restoration is rather simple. The following list details possible problems and solutions:

A system being used as a distribution point fails   After restoring the system, simply redistribute the packages to that individual system to repopulate it.

An NT controller being used as a logon point fails   After the controller is reinstalled, it will automatically become a functional logon point again.

A NetWare server being used as a logon point fails   Re-create the logon point on the restored system using the SMS Administrator Console. You may want to ensure that the same volume is available on the restored system as was used originally.

Diagnosing and Resolving Site-to-Site Communication Problems

Problems that occur during site-to-site connection generally involve improper configuration of addresses or senders, as listed here:

Send requests are not being serviced   Use dumpsend to determine the priority and destination of the request. Make sure that an address is available for the time and priority of the request.

Senders cannot connect to other sites   Confirm that the sender is attempting a connection by viewing the sender.log file with SMS Trace. Force the sender to start using SMS Service Manager. Connection failure is most likely due to an incorrect account or destination server entered in the address settings.

Choosing the Appropriate Diagnostic Tool

1. Which SMS tool is used to capture and analyze network traffic?

2. Which SMS tool would best identify rogue DHCP servers?

3. The _____ utility extracts the contents of send-request files.

4. Connectivity to the WBEM repository can be confirmed by using _____.

5. Multiple log files can be viewed simultaneously using _____.

6. Details of status messages are read using the _____.

Diagnosing and Resolving SMS Site System Installation Problems

7. If the installation of a primary site server fails, the _____ file will be found on server.

8. A primary site server requires a _____ partition with at least _____ of free space.

9. Each SMS Administrator Console connection requires _____ SQL user connections.

10. The SMS service account must be a member of the _____ group.

11. True/False: When installing a secondary site server the installation partition is automatically converted to NTFS.

12. The _____ file details client attempts to connect to CAPs.

13. True/False: Only primary domain controllers can be logon points.

Diagnosing and Resolving Client Installation Problems

14. The installation of an SMS client requires a minimum of _____ of free disk space.

15. True/False: A system that is not within the site boundaries can only be installed as a client manually.

Diagnosing and Resolving Software Distribution Problems

16. When a distribution point is located on a Novell Directory Services(NDS)–based NetWare 4.11 server, you must install the _____ client on the site server.

17. When a distribution point is located on a bindery-based Novell 3.12 server, you must install _____ on the site server.

18. Software distribution is primarily a function of the _____.

Diagnosing and Resolving Inventory Collection Problems

19. The installation of the hardware inventory agent is recorded in the _____ file.

20. 20.True/False: Schedules for the site from which you installed the agent always determine the agent execution schedule.

21. True/False: If a file requested to be collected exceeds the size limits configured by the administrator the file will not be collected.

Diagnosing and Resolving Remote Control Problems

22. True/False: Permission to remote control is granted automatically to members of SMS Admins.

23. True/False: The Permitted Viewers list is managed individually on each client.

24. How many protocols can the remote control agent be bound to on a client?

25. When attempting to remote control a client on a remote segment, NetBIOS name resolution can be performed using either a _____ server or a _____ file.

26. 26.True/False: The administrator's system can attempt to contact a client's remote control agent on up to eight protocols.

Diagnosing and Resolving Software Metering Problems

27. True/False: Licensing is still enforced for SMS clients that disconnect their machines from the network.

28. True/False: All Windows-based clients can support software metering.

29. Data Summarization occurs by default every _____ hours.

30. Programs can be identified by either their name as it appears in Explorer, or by _____ information.

31. The _____ file records the activities of the software metering agent.

Diagnosing and Resolving SNMP Integration Problems

32. True/False: Before an SNMP trap message can be generated, a condition must be entered in the Windows NT Event Log.

33. True/False: The primary site server must be included as a trap destination.

34. The SNMP Event to Trap Translator agent can be installed only on _____-based computers.

35. True/False: The installation of the SNMP Event to Trap Translator agent does not install the Windows NT SNMP agent.

Restoring an SMS Site

36. True/False: When restoring an SMS database to a new SQL server, the new SQL server must have the same machine name as the original SQL server.

37. True/False: When restoring a primary site server, it must have the same computer name as the original system.

38. The _____ file holds the current site settings.

39. True/False: When restoring the SMS registry keys, all SMS services must be stopped.

40. True/False: Packages can be resent to individual distribution points.

41. If a new backup domain controller is added to an existing domain where Windows NT Logon Installation is enabled, it will automatically become an SMS logon point.

Diagnosing and Resolving Site-to-Site Communication Problems

42. The sending of data between sites can be restricted, based on _____ and _____.

43. The sender thread can be started and stopped manually using the _____.

44. The most effective way to troubleshoot site-to-site connectivity is by viewing the _____ file.

S A M P L E   T E S T

6-1 Example Company is hosting a conference with visitors from other companies. Attendees will be using their own laptop systems to collect e-mail and access the Internet. IP addresses will be assigned using DHCP and access will be controlled using a Proxy Server. The administrator wants to ensure that none of the visitors use Network Monitor while attached to the corporate network.

Which of the following tools should the administrator use?

A. Network Monitor

B. Network Monitor Control Tool

C. WBEMtest

D. Software Metering Manager

6-2 Example Company has three domains: DOM1, DOM2, and DOM3. DOM3 and DOM2 trust DOM1. The administrator has installed SMS on a member server in DOM2 using an account from DOM1 as the SMS service account.

When the administrator later enables Windows NT Logon Discovery, controllers in which domain's controllers will become logon points by default?

A. DOM1

B. DOM2

C. DOM3

D. No domains are listed by default

6-3 The administrator has determined from status messages that the installation of a secondary site has failed. Which of the following items should the administrator confirm?

A. The SMS service account is a member of Domain Admins.

B. The SMS service account has the right to log on as a service.

C. There is at least 1GB of free NTFS space on the target server.

D. There is at least 100MB of free disk space on the system partition.

6-4   Example Company's administrator is attempting to create a new distribution point on a Novell NetWare 4.11 server. After installing GSNW on the site server he created the appropriate NetWare NDS Site System Connection Account and assigned it Admin rights to the server's volume.

The creation of the DP fails. What is the most probable reason for the failure?

A. The NetWare volume specified is not formatted with NTFS.

B. NetWare servers cannot be used as DPs.

C. The GSNW service is not started on the site server.

D. The IntraNetWare client was not loaded.

6-5   The administrator wants to review each of the client's `liccli.log` files. The administrator specifies that the file should be collected from all clients in the site. The site includes Windows for Workgroups, Windows 95, and Windows NT clients. The maximum client log settings are determined by the default on all client machines. The maximum file collection size is also found in the default settings.

When reviewing the collected files using the Resource Explorer, the administrator notices that many clients did not report a `liccli.log` file, even though their software inventory agent ran successfully.

Which of the following reasons is the most probable?

A. The client's `liccli.log` file size exceeded the maximum file collection size.

B. The clients had insufficient disk space to generate a copy of the file.

C. The permissions on the client's CAP prevented reporting the file.

D. Not all clients in the site are running the software metering agent.

6-6 Example Company's administrator has confirmed using Network Monitor that client's are properly generating trap messages. However, trap messages are being directed to the incorrect SNMP manager.

What must the administrator do to direct the traps to the proper destination?

    A. Reinstall the SNMP Event to Trap Translator agent.

    B. Modify the trap destination in the NT SNMP agent settings.

    C. Rename the site server's domain as Public.

    D. Install a WINS server.

6-7 SMS clients in Example Company's SMS site are exclusively running Windows NT workstation 4 or Windows NT Server 4. Some of the workstations are running both TCP/IP and NetBEUI; others are running TCP/IP alone.

The administrator's workstation is running only TCP/IP. The remote control agent was installed with the default advanced features enabled.

Which of the following statements is true?

    A. All clients will bind the remote control agent to TCP/IP.

    B. All clients will bind the remote control agent to the first protocol installed.

    C. The installation of the remote control agent will fail on systems with multiple protocols.

    D. To be able to remote control all clients, the administrator must be at a computer that has both protocols installed.

6-8 Although software metering has been enabled for all clients in Example Company's site, license limits are not being enforced for any products. The administrator has checked the clients' `liccli.log` files and has verified that licenses are being granted but limits are not being enforced.

Which two of the following could cause this problem?

A. Real-time license verification is not enabled.

B. The enforcement of license limits was not specified for registered products.

C. All products have been excluded.

D. Licensing won't be enforced until a trend has been calculated.

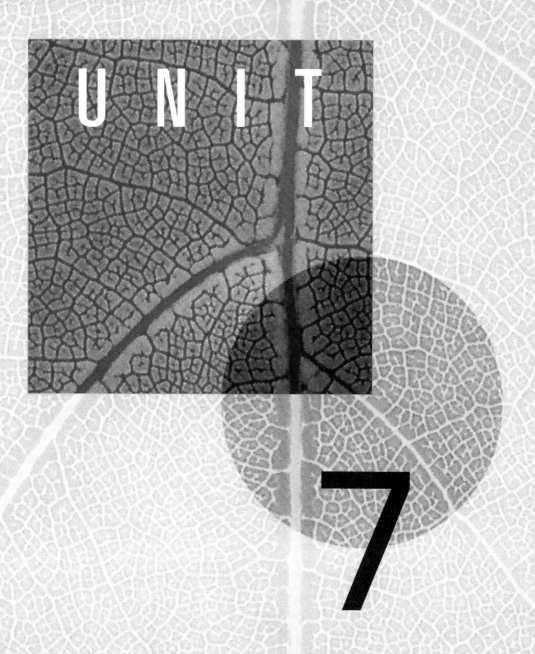

UNIT

7

Final Exam

FINAL EXAM

7-1 Example Company's administrator is planning to install a primary site server on a member server in DomainX.

Which of the following actions will result if the Express Setup method is used to perform the installation?

  A. The Windows NT Logon Discovery method will be enabled.

  B. The Windows NT Logon Installation method will be enabled.

  C. An SMSLOGON share point will be created on the primary site server.

  D. All domain controllers in DomainX will receive SMSLOGON share points.

  E. All user logon scripts, with the exception of the administrator's, will be directed to the `smsls.bat` batch file.

7-2 After installing a new primary site server, the administrator realizes that he has used the same site code as that of another site in the hierarchy to which he wants to attach.

Which of the following steps must the administrator perform before adding the site to the hierarchy?

  A. Edit the `Site_Definition` section of the site control file to reflect a unique site code.

  B. Run SMS Setup, and choose the option to Reset the Site; then enter a unique site code.

  C. Reinstall the primary site server using a unique site code.

  D. Do nothing. Non-unique site codes can be used as long as they do not have direct parent-child relationships.

7-3 Example Company's administrator determined that no more than eight SMS administrators would ever require simultaneous access. Just to be safe, however, she configured the SQL Server to support 10 user connections.

SMS administrators later report that they cannot consistently gain access via the SMS Administrator Console and that various components are shown to be in a critical state.

Which of the following steps should the administrator perform to rectify the problem?

A. Increase the number of SQL user connections to 50 by resetting the site.

B. Increase the number of SQL user connections to 100 by resetting the site.

C. Increase the number of SQL user connections to 50 using SQL Enterprise Manager.

D. Increase the number of SQL user connections to 100 using SQL Enterprise Manager.

7-4 Example Company currently has three separate SMS sites. S01 and S02 are SMS 1.2 primary sites, and S03 is an SMS 2 primary site.

Which of the following parent-child relationships can be established without upgrading any sites?

A. S01 can be a parent to S03.

B. S02 can be a parent to S03.

C. S03 can be a parent to S01.

D. None.

7-5 Which of the following statements are true regarding upgrading SMS 1.2 sites to SMS 2 sites?

A. The topmost site in the hierarchy must be upgraded first.

B. The bottommost sites in the hierarchy must be upgraded first.

C. Upgrading of a secondary site can be initiated from its parent site.

D. Upgrading of a secondary site can be initiated locally at the secondary site.

E. SMS 1.2 secondary sites can be upgraded to SMS 2 primary sites during the upgrade process.

```
┌─────────────────────────────┐
│       F I N A L   E X A M      │
└─────────────────────────────┘
```

7-6 During an attempt to administer a secondary site using the SMS Administrator Console, the connection fails. The administrator reenters the name of the secondary site server but encounters the same results.

What is the most likely cause of the connection failure?

A. SQL Server is not running on the secondary site server.

B. SQL Server is configured for an insufficient number of user connections.

C. The SMS Executive service is not running on the secondary site server.

D. The administrator is connecting to the wrong site.

7-7 Which of the following statements regarding senders are correct?

A. The courier sender does not require configuration.

B. Senders can only reside on Windows NT servers.

C. Only one sender of each type is permitted per site.

D. Senders pass data to the receiving site server's SMS_SITE share.

7-8 Which of the following systems can be used as logon servers?

A. Windows NT Primary Domain Controllers

B. Windows NT Backup Domain Controllers

C. Windows NT member servers

D. Novell NetWare 3.*x* (Bindery) servers

E. Novell NetWare 4.*x* (NDS) servers

7-9 Which of the following shares is the primary point of communication between SMS clients and servers?

A. CAP_SXX

B. NETLOGON

C. REPL$

D. SMS_SITE

E. SMS_SXX

7-10   Which of the following steps must be performed to change the parent of a secondary site?

    A. Detach from the parent site.

    B. Delete the secondary site.

    C. Uninstall the secondary site.

    D. Reinstall the secondary site.

7-11   Example Company's administrator frequently attaches her laptop to different points of the corporate network. A different IP address is assigned from a DHCP server within each subnet.

What must she do to ensure that her computer is not installed into different sites because of the different site boundaries?

    A. Use a static IP address.

    B. Use traveling mode.

    C. Disable Windows NT Logon Installation.

    D. Disable Network Discovery.

7-12   Which of the following events will occur by default if Heartbeat Discovery is disabled?

    A. All discovery data will be deleted from the SMS database after 1 month.

    B. All discovery data will be deleted from the SMS database after 3 months.

FINAL EXAM

C. All discovery data for systems where nobody logs on will be deleted after 1 on month.

D. All discovery data for systems where nobody logs on will be deleted after 3 months.

7-13 Which of the following statements about incorporating SMS into a NetWare-based network are true?

A. The SMS Executive runs as an NLM on NetWare servers.

B. Both NetWare 3.*x* and 4.*x* servers can be used as site systems.

C. The Primary Site Server must run the Gateway Services for NetWare or the IntraNetWare client.

D. NetWare volumes can be used as both client access points and distribution points (DPs).

7-14 Which of the following thread or services is responsible for retrieving data held at NetWare-based CAPs?

A. Inbox Manager

B. Inbox Manager Assistant

C. Inventory Data Loader

D. Inventory Processor

7-15 Example Company's administrator wants to edit the SMS_DEF.MOF in order to collect additional hardware details.

Which of the following tools will allow her to edit the file most simply?

A. MOF Manager

B. Microsoft Word

C. SMS Administrator Console

D. Hinv32.exe

7-16   Which of the following client logs should be viewed to determine the proper execution of the 32-bit Hardware Inventory Agent?

    A. `Inhinv32.log`

    B. `Hinv32.log`

    C. `Inventry.log`

    D. `Cqmgr32.log`

7-17   By default, the Software Inventory Agent is configured only to inventory files with which extensions?

    A. `.txt`

    B. `.com`

    C. `.bat`

    D. `.exe`

7-18   Example Company's administrator has enabled both user and group discovery in addition to NDS Logon Discovery. The administrator notes later that none of the NetWare users and groups are being discovered.

Which of the following steps should the administrator take?

    A. Enable NDS Logon Installation.

    B. Change the site boundaries to include the proper IPX network numbers.

    C. Change the polling interval for user and group discovery.

    D. Do nothing.

7-19   Example Company's employees are permitted to play approved computer games during lunchtime.

Which of the following steps should the administrator perform to ensure that users who attempt to run programs during none approved times are denied?

    A. Install the games on an NTFS partition of the server.

    B. Enabling auditing of File and Object Access.

    C. Assign access to a "game" account.

    D. Restrict logon times for the "game" account to lunch hours only.

    E. Configure permitted times for the games in the Software Metering Console.

7-20 The administrator has noticed that software-metering reports include many in-house applications that should not be metered.

What is the most effective way to ensure that the use of in-house applications is not recorded?

    A. Disable the software-metering agent for clients using in-house applications.

    B. Exclude the in-house applications.

    C. Restrict access to the in-house applications.

    D. Create a report filter to exclude the in-house applications.

7-21 Which of the following statements regarding callback are true?

    A. Domain Admins receive the highest callback priority.

    B. Callback priority can be set based on user, group, or computer.

    C. By default, callback requests expire after 30 minutes.

    D. NetWare clients do not receive callback notifications.

7-22 What are the minimum bandwidth requirements for remote control?

    A. 14.4kbps

    B. 28.8kbps

C. 56kbps

D. 10mbps

7-23 Which of the following statements about remote control is true?

A. Remote control is supported only for 32-bit Windows clients.

B. Only administrators can be members of the Permitted Viewers list.

C. Remote control sessions are logged in the NT Security Event Log.

D. Remote control clients must have 150MHz or faster processors.

7-24 Which of the following database options is enabled for the SMS database by default?

A. Read Only

B. DBO Use Only

C. Single User

D. Truncate Log on Checkpoint

7-25 An SMS administrator has noticed that some of the collections cannot be modified and have a small lock showing as an icon.

What is the most likely cause?

A. The administrator was removed from the SMS Admins group.

B. The collections originated at a parent site.

C. The database has been corrupted.

D. The SQL Server is configured for insufficient open objects.

7-26 After purchasing a new SQL Server, the SMS administrator ran SMS setup on the existing primary site server to enter the new SQL information.

F I N A L   E X A M

After restarting, the administrator is unable to connect to the SQL Server via the SMS Administrator Console.

What should the administrator do to fix the problem?

    A. Modify the SQL information in the registry manually.

    B. Increase the tempdb database on the new SQL Server.

    C. Reinstall the SMS provider.

    D. Move the SQL databases to the new server.

7-27   When the database maintenance task Backup the Site Server is enabled, which of the following items are backed up?

    A. The SMS database and log

    B. The Metering database and log

    C. The SMS key in the registry

    D. The SMS directory on the site server

7-28   After a crash of Example Company's primary site server, the administrator has restored the SMS directory and registry keys to a new computer.

The SQL Server housing the SMS databases was unaffected.

When the administrator attempts to restart the new computer, the SMS services fail to start.

Which of the following are possible causes?

    A. The new computer has a different processor type.

    B. The new computer has a different domain name.

    C. The new computer has a different machine name.

    D. The new computer has a different IP address.

7-29   The SMS administrator of the Central Site wants to delegate administrative responsibility of a secondary site to another user. After setting the proper class and instance security rights, to which NT group should the user be added?

   A. SMS Admins

   B. Domain Admins

   C. Administrators

   D. Server Operators

7-30   The SMS administrator wants to permit members of a certain NT group to remote control all systems except the accounting computers.

   Which of the following steps should the administrator perform?

   A. Create a collection containing only accounting computers.

   B. Using instance security settings deny remote control access to the desired NT group.

   C. Create a collection containing all systems except accounting computers.

   D. Using instance security settings grant remote control access to the desired NT group.

   E. Using class security settings grant remote control access to the desired NT group.

7-31   Which of the following statements about SMS client installation is true?

   A. Clients install their core components from CAPs.

   B. Clients install their core components from DPs.

   C. Installation of an NT client requires an administrator to be logged on locally.

   D. Installation is always initiated by some form of logon.

FINAL EXAM

7-32   Which of the following statements about client assignment are true?

    A. Clients can be assigned to a single site only.

    B. Clients must be assigned to be discovered.

    C. Client assignment is determined by the client.

    D. Client assignment is based on either IP subnet or IPX network number.

7-33   Example Company's administrator has installed an SMS primary site server on a member server in DomainX, using Express Setup. All clients in DomainX have the same IP subnet. After installation, the administrator enables the option to automatically configure the logon scripts under the settings for Windows NT Logon Discovery.

Based on this information, which of the following statements are true?

    A. SMS logon points will be created on all controllers in DomainX.

    B. SMS logon points will be created on all member servers used as site systems in DomainX.

    C. All supported clients in DomainX will be discovered upon logon.

    D. All supported clients in DomainX will be installed upon logon.

7-34   Under which of the following conditions will the installation of SMS client software be terminated?

    A. The client is unassigned.

    B. The client's connection speed is 40kbps or less.

    C. The client does not have an NTFS partition.

    D. The client does not have sufficient free disk space.

7-35 After enabling both the hardware and software inventory agents, the administrator forces an update from one of the clients. Even though the agents appear to have installed, neither hardware nor software information is being seen via the SMS Administrator Console.

Which of the following is the most likely cause?

    A. The administrator has not waited long enough.

    B. The client's time is not synchronized with the site server's time.

    C. The SQL Server is down.

    D. The client computer has not rebooted.

7-36 The SMS administrator has created a custom `IDMIF` file to collect information about employees' cell phones, including model and phone number.

The `IDMIF` file was placed in the site server's `SMS\Inventry.box` folder.

Although clients claim to have entered information, the administrator cannot find the IDMIF data using Resource Explorer.

Which of the following is the most likely cause?

    A. The Hardware Inventory Agent is not enabled.

    B. The Software Inventory Agent is not enabled.

    C. The IDMIF file is corrupt.

    D. Resource Explorer does not report IDMIF file data.

7-37 The administrator has learned of a new virus called the Mean Green Witch. It is supposed to affect all NT computers in the world at the same time, exactly 2:00 PM Eastern Standard Time (EST). In order to inoculate all systems in the organization, each system must execute a virus scan at the same time, one minute before the virus takes effect.

FINAL EXAM

What should the administrator do when setting the advertisement schedule for the execution of the antivirus program?

    A. Set the program to execute at 1:59 PM on all systems.

    B. Set the program to execute at 6:59 PM on all systems.

    C. Select the Greenwich Mean Time (GMT) option.

    D. Make the advertisement mandatory.

7-38 The administrator has created a collection based on a query, which locates systems that have not yet been upgraded to the latest service pack.

After awhile, the administrator refreshes the collection window and is surprised to see some of the members of the collection are systems he recently upgraded.

What is the probable cause for the systems still being members of the collection?

    A. The administrator has not updated the collection.

    B. The administrator has not rerun the query.

    C. The administrator has deleted the original query.

    D. The upgrade of the systems was not successful.

7-39 The administrator created a package containing a service pack of NT for Alpha-based systems using a package definition file. When advertising the program, he accidentally sent it as a mandatory assignment to the All Systems collection.

What will happen when clients that are of the wrong processor type or operating system learn of the advertisement?

    A. The advertisement will not appear to clients with the wrong platform.

    B. The advertisement will not appear to clients with the wrong operating system.

    C. The advertisement will run because it is mandatory.

    D. The program will fail and report an error.

7-40   Example Company has a single SMS site. The site spans five NT domains and three IP subnets. The network group is complaining that distribution of large packages to distribution points is occurring too frequently during peak hours.

Which of the following steps can the administrator perform to reduce the impact of software distribution to remote DPs during business hours?

  A. Create a distribution point group containing the remote DPs.

  B. Set address restrictions to limit the hours when sending to the DPs is permitted.

  C. Set address restrictions to limit the bandwidth usage when sending packages to the DPs.

  D. Wait until off-peak hours to distribute the package.

7-41   The SMS administrator has advertised a program to a collection containing 10 systems. Although a full day has passed, the advertisement has not appeared on many of the systems.

Which of the following could be the reason for the advertisement not appearing?

  A. The client's time is not synchronized with that of the SQL Server.

  B. The client's operating system is not supported.

  C. The client's platform is not supported.

  D. The user has insufficient permissions to run the program.

7-42   Example Company's administrator wants to ensure that it is in compliance with the licensing policies for a particular package. The administrator imports the license policy provided with the package to configure the settings.

After running a report, the administrator realizes that they are exceeding the number of licenses permitted; however, no clients are being denied.

Which of the following reasons would account for the clients not being denied when the license limit was exceeded?

    A. The software metering client agent was not enabled.

    B. The agent was not configured to force real-time license verification.

    C. The option not to enforce license limits until a trend is calculated was selected.

    D. The option to enforce license limits for the product was not selected.

7-43 Which of the following utilities will be able to inform the administrator if the SQL Server stops unexpectedly?

    A. SNMP Event to Trap Translator

    B. Network Monitor

    C. Health Monitor

    D. Performance Monitor

7-44 Which of the following are requirements of the computer used as the SMS Installer reference computer?

    A. The computer must run Windows 3.*x* or greater.

    B. The computer must run Windows 95 or greater.

    C. The computer must be an SMS server.

    D. The computer must be an SMS client.

7-45 The SMS administrator wants to control SMS traffic between sites. Which of the following restrictions can the administrator place on addresses between sites?

    A. Traffic can be limited to that of a particular priority or above.

    B. Traffic can be limited to that of a particular collection.

    C. Traffic can be limited to a percentage of available bandwidth.

    D. Traffic can be limited to certain times of the day.

APPENDIX

Unit 1

Study Questions

Designing a Microsoft Systems Management Server (SMS) Site

1. True

2. True

3. False

   Explanation: Software licensing is monitored using the software metering feature of SMS 2.

4. False

   Explanation: It is best to implement only the necessary features in each site in order to avoid unnecessary overhead and complications.

5. 1.1

6. SQL

7. False

   Explanation: Although it would certainly benefit you to understand SQL syntax, you can use many predefined queries and create new ones using simple relational operators.

8. Query

9. Software metering

10. Windows

11. Monitor

12. Discovery

13. Trace

14. Resource

15. Collection

16. Subnets

17. Primary, parent

18. True

19. Secondary

Explanation: Secondary sites do not have direct access to a SQL database.

20. False

Explanation: Secondary sites are always child sites, but child sites can be either primary or secondary sites.

21. Central

22. Sender

Explanation: Senders are used when reporting information from a child site to its parent and also when sending advertisements or packages from a parent site to a child.

23. Windows NT Server 4 with Service Pack 4.

24. Secondary

25. False

Explanation: A child site that is also a primary site could also be a parent site.

26. SMS client access points

27. Component

28. Distribution

Designing an SMS Site Hierarchy

29. True

30. 50

31. 10,000 to 30,000

32. Unlimited, but note that the hierarchy is best kept as flat as possible.

33. True

34. False

Explanation: The determination of site membership is independent of domain membership. It is based solely on site assignment.

35. True

36. Courier

37. True

38. 28.8

39. True

40. False

Explanation: The central site should be located at the administrative center of the organization, which is not necessarily the same as the physical center of the network infrastructure.

41. Primary

42. False

Explanation: A child site can have only one parent site.

43. 50

Explanation: The maximum of 50 child sites reporting to a single parent is a recommendation based on performance.

44. False

Explanation: The site hierarchy is dictated by many factors. Although the physical network infrastructure is certainly considered when determining the site hierarchy, it does not direct the logical relationships formed between sites.

45. True

Explanation: You can include multiple language versions in the same hierarchy, but not all reported information will be translated. Give an example.

46. True

47. True

48. False

Planning a Security Strategy for SMS Servers

49. You must establish trust relationships between the domains.

50. SMS Service

51. SMS Remote Service

52. SQL Server

53. Standard, integrated

54. False

Explanation: The SMS Client Software Installation Account is used when the user logged on at the client computer does not have permission to install advertised software.

55. Web-based Enterprise Management (WBEM)

56. Class, instance

Planning for Interoperability and Upgrades

57. False

Explanation: SMS 2 does not support Macintosh, MS-DOS, or OS/2 clients. Additionally, the Package Command Manager (PCM) is not supported in SMS 2.

58. False

Explanation: SMS 1.2 sites can be managed only using the SMS Administrator program.

Sample Test

1-1 A, C, and D

Explanation: Novell NetWare 4.11 servers can perform any site system roles associated with NetWare NDS volumes. Note that none of the roles that can be assigned to a Novell NetWare server requires services to be run at the Novell NetWare server itself.

1-2 B

Explanation: Part of a Windows NT Server system, component servers run various SMS 2 services instead of, or in addition to, their being run on the site server.

1-3 B

Explanation: The required objective is met because the administrators will be able to distribute packages from the central/parent site in Miami to each of the child sites.

However, the desired objective is not met. For maximum performance a single site should not exceed 3000 users. The administrator should divide the Miami location into two separate sites.

1-4 A

Explanation: Although you can perform resource discovery on a per domain basis, it can generate undesired traffic when a domain is distributed across multiple subnets. By identifying resources within each subnet, the administrator can control the impact the discovery process will have on the network. Once each of the subnets has been searched, all of the SMS objects in the domain will be discovered.

1-5   D

Explanation: Senders by nature are bidirectional, so if the child sites can report information to Miami it is apparent that the required senders are in place. To direct information via the senders to the child sites, Miami requires an address for each site to be created.

1-6   A and D

Explanation: SMS 1.2 sites can coexist with SMS 2 sites, but they must be below the SMS 2 sites in the hierarchy.

1-7   D

Explanation: Network Trace can generate an image showing the relationships among SMS site systems. The information that it uses is based on details collected using Network Discovery.

1-8   D

Explanation: The site in Tampa is a secondary site. Secondary sites cannot have child sites that report to them. Because the solution fails to link the new location to the SMS hierarchy, neither the required nor the desired objective is met.

1-9   A

Explanation: The number of users at the new location does not justify forming a new site. Moreover, because the Tampa site is a secondary site it could not support child sites. By including the new location within the site boundaries of the Tampa site, the administrators in Tampa will be able to manage the resources, so the required result is met. The desired result is also met, as the Tampa site reports the information it collects to its parent site, the headquarters in Miami.

1-10   D

Explanation: In SMS 2, permissions are controlled using the SMS Administrator Console. Although groups are created and managed User Manager for Domains, the security rights assigned to the group are managed using the SMS Administrator Console.

1-11 B

Explanation: SMS 2 is not a cure-all for every problem you may encounter. Although you could track Internet use with Network Monitor, it would hardly be an effective way of doing this. Additionally, although software metering can control Internet access times, it cannot identify which websites users are visiting. The function of Network Trace has nothing to do with tracking users; rather, it provides a graphical representation of the links between SMS site systems and the physical network.

A proxy server is the only viable option, as it can control both the permitted access times and locations.

1-12 A, C, and D

Explanation: Both the SMS client access point and distribution point would be required elements for the advertising and delivery of the package. The logon point would also be required to discover the Novell NetWare 3.12 clients.

1-13 A and B

Explanation: Both SMS client access points and distribution points are roles that can be assigned to Windows NT shares. Although a logon point may actually use a share, the role is assigned to the NT controller or NetWare server, not to the share itself. Only a Windows NT Server can be used as a software metering server.

1-14 A

Explanation: The central site must always be a primary site to fulfill its primary responsibility of reporting the information to the SQL database.

The central site is the site highest in the SMS hierarchy; therefore it could not be installed in the middle of the logical site hierarchy. Also, although the central site might be located in the middle of the physical network, nothing states that it must be. Generally, the central site should be located where the head SMS administrators are.

There is no requirement to install the central site in a separate NT domain.

1-15 D

Explanation: The courier sender can be used when there is little or no connectivity between sites.

1-16   A and C

Explanation: SMS 2 includes two senders that were not a part of SMS 1.2. Don't confuse the new RAS (SNA) sender with the SNA sender found in SMS 1.2. If a site requires SNA connectivity, then it should be upgraded to SMS 2.

The courier sender is unique to SMS 2 and cannot be used in conjunction with SMS 1.2 sites.

1-17   A, B, C, and D

Explanation: All of the answers are correct. Only primary sites can be parent sites, as they need to record information about their child sites and themselves into the SQL database. In a multilayer site hierarchy the parent sites in the middle layers would also be child sites of the site above them in the hierarchy. The central site is the parent of all sites in the layer immediately below it.

1-18   B, C, and D

Explanation: SMS 2 is significantly more flexible in its approach than version 1.2, in which sites were made up of one or more domains. SMS 2 boundaries are defined by subnets. This allows a single domain to be divided into multiple SMS sites.

In SMS 2, *subnets*, which refers to IP subnets or IPX network numbers, define the boundaries.

1-19   B and C

Explanation: Membership in the Administrators group ensures that the SMS Service Account will not encounter any security restrictions. The right to log on as a service is required to allow the SMS Service Account to be validated remotely, independent of an interactive user.

1-20   A and D

Explanation: Primary sites must record the information they collect into a SQL database; however, a single SQL Server can house multiple databases. Although primary sites can have one or more child sites below it, they are not required to have sites below them.

Unit 2

Study Questions

Installing, Configuring, and Modifying a Primary Site Server

1. False

   Explanation: Only a Microsoft SQL Server can be used as the SMS database server.

2. False

   Explanation: The Microsoft SQL Server must be accessible to the primary site server, but it does not have to be installed on the same computer.

3. 6.5, 7

4. Express

5. True

6. Database, log

7. False

   Explanation: Although you can assign the SMS database to a preexisting device, this will cause all objects on the device to be lost. You should try to avoid doing this.

8. SMSDATA, SMSLOG

9. True

10. Enterprise

11. ALTER

12. Standard, integrated, and mixed

13. False

Explanation: The SQL Server can be located in either the same domain as the primary site server or in a domain that trusts the primary site server's domain. When standard security is used, the domain membership is not relevant.

14. Tempdb

15. 1500

16. 4.01 or later with SP1

17. DEC Alpha

18. 1000

19. False

    Explanation: Site codes should be maintained as unique throughout a hierarchy, but it is the administrator's responsibility to ensure they do not get duplicated.

20. Three

21. False

    Explanation: The site domain is the name of the domain of which the site server is a member. The site server's domain is not necessarily the same as that of SQL Server.

22. SMS service

23. True

24. NT

25. Five

Installing a Secondary Site Server

26. SMS CD, Secondary Site Wizard

27. True

28. True

29. False

Explanation: The software metering service is an optional component that is not installed by default at a secondary site server.

30. Asynchronous RAS

31. True

32. SMS_SITE

33. True

Configuring Site System Roles

34. Windows NT

35. Component

36. True

37. Bindery, NDS

38. Domain

39. Distribution

40. False

Explanation: The workload on the site server can be reduced by not using it as a distribution point.

41. True

42. Client access

43. Client access

44.　NT servers, NT shares, volumes

45.　Windows NT 4, 4

Configuring an SMS Site Hierarchy

46.　Addresses

47.　True

　　Explanation: By configuring multiple addresses to a single site, you can increase the data capacity and provide redundancy.

48.　True

49.　Lowest

50.　False

　　Explanation: The latest address created is always given the lowest precedence by default.

51.　Standard

52.　Asynchronous, SNA, ISDN, X.25

53.　Courier

54.　One

55.　Primary sites

56.　Set Parent Site

57.　SQL Server Enterprise Manager

58.　False

　　Explanation: A site can contain a combination of hardware platforms used as site systems. The only stipulations are that you must install the binaries for both Intel and Alpha platforms during installation or add them afterward by rerunning the Setup program. Also, only Intel-based systems can be used as software metering servers.

Sample Test

2-1   D or E

Explanation: The SMS database server must run Microsoft SQL 6.5 with SP5, or Microsoft SQL 7.The reliance on extended stored procedures and other proprietary features makes this necessary.

2-2   D

Explanation: Although using Express Setup would install all mandatory and optional SMS components, the presence of an existing copy of SQL Server on the computer would disallow the use of this kind of setup.

2-3   C

Explanation: Although implementing the plan would meet the objective, any objects on the accounting devices would be dropped in the process. This therefore would not be a desirable solution.

2-4   D

Explanation: Four devices will be required. By default the devices would be SMSDATA, SMSLOG, LIC_DATA, and LIC_LOG.

2-5   A and B

Explanation: Standard, integrated, or mixed security modes could be used. If integrated security were used, then the SQL Server's domain would need to trust the primary site server's domain. The operative word in answers C and D is "must." Standard mode does not require the trust to exist.

2-6   A

Explanation: Tempdb is used as workspace for all SQL databases when responding to queries using `GROUP BY`, `ORDER BY`, or `DISTINCT` or involving temporary objects such as server-side cursors or temporary tables.

2-7   B and D

Explanation: The installation program does not confirm site code uniqueness. If the administrator improperly assigns the same site code to two sites, If this occurs, it will not be possible to establish parent-child relationships between them. You must use three-character alphanumeric site codes.

2-8   A, B, and D

Explanation: When installing a secondary site, you need to provide the secondary site's site code, site name, and site domain. You also need to provide the following information about the parent site: site code, parent site server name, and type of sender to use when communicating with the parent site.

The name of the domain where the primary site is installed is not required when installing a secondary site.

2-9   A

Explanation: Once a site code has been established, the only way to change it is to reinstall the site. Neither SQL Enterprise Manager nor the SQL Administrator Console can be used to effectively change site codes. The `codegen.exe` program is fictitious.

2-10   A

Explanation: The administrators access the SQL Server via the SMS provider. The SMS provider requires only a single account that will be used on behalf of the administrator. The access permissions of administrators are controlled individually by the WBEM protocol, which exposes only the objects to which access is granted.

2-11   A

Explanation: Installing a secondary site automatically installs both the standard sender and courier sender. Although the secondary site is configured with an address that is directed to its parent site, an address for the secondary site must be manually created at the parent site.

2-12   B

Explanation: Novell NetWare 4.11 servers require that NetWare NDS Support be installed on the site server in order to use them as logon points. If the question had asked about Novell NetWare 3.12 servers, then NetWare Bindery Support would have been required. The SMS Administrator Console NLM does not exist.

2-13   B and D

Explanation: It is important to remember that the sender only defines the logical path between sites. The addresses define when and how to use a specific sender.

2-14 A

Explanation: SMS only supports the use of Microsoft SQL Server 6.5 with SP 5 or Microsoft SQL Server 7. Both Intel and DEC Alpha platforms are supported by Microsoft SQL Server. Although the SMS provider can be placed on the SQL Server, it is not a requirement. The SMS Setup program only changes the logical pointers to the SQL Server; it does not physically move the database. SQL Enterprise Manager could be used to move the physical database.

2-15 All of the above.

Explanation: All of the responses are correct. The workload on the primary site server can be reduced by relocating distribution points on other systems and by moving the SMS provider to the SQL Server. Redirecting the processing of child site data to another site will reduce the processing load. Having fewer subnets in the site boundaries will reduce the site server's area of responsibility.

Unit 3

Study Questions

Configuring Software and Hardware Inventory Collection for a Site

1. Discovered

2. Site

3. Hardware inventory

4. True

5. False

   Explanation: Enabling the hardware inventory agent for a site installs the agent on both 32- and 16-bit Windows-based clients.

6. False

   Explanation: Clients report collected inventory to a client access point.

7. Hours, days, weeks

8. Full

9. `Hinv`

10. `Mofcomp.exe`

11. `Hinv32.exe`

12. `Hinvdat.hic`

    Explanation: The extension stands for hardware inventory complete.

13. `Hinvdat.hid`

    Explanation: The extension stands for hardware inventory delta (changes).

14. 3, 2

15. `.exe`

16. False

    Explanation: Although wildcards can be used (`*.com` or `win*.*`), it is not permitted to use `*.*` independently of a qualifier.

17. True

18. False

    Explanation: File collection does not *move* files but rather just *copies* selected files.

19. 10

    Explanation: This space requirement is an estimate that will vary depending on the amount of files to be collected from the clients. The client is responsible for creating a copy of the files to be collected before transferring them to the client access point.

Managing Inventory Data

20. Resource Explorer

21. SMS_def.mof

22. DMTF

23. True

24. False

Explanation: Both IDMIFs and NOIDMIFs extend the default settings held in the SMS_def.mof.

25. Classes

Distributing Software

26. SMS Installer

27. Reference

28. Target

29. False

Explanation: Although it must be installed first on a site server, the reference computers do not need to be site servers but simply Windows-based computers.

30. False

Explanation: When a package definition file exists, you can import it using the Create Package from Definition Wizard; however, a definition file is not a requirement to distribute a package.

31. This Package Does Not Contain Any Files.

32. Always Use a Compressed Version of the Source.

33. SMSPKGD

34. Medium

35. False

Explanation: There is no requirement to assign a preferred sender. If one is not designated as preferred, the system will choose any available sender in order of priority.

36. Program

37. Start in

Explanation: The Start in parameter is located in the program's General tab.

38. After running

Explanation: The After running parameter is located in the program's General tab.

39. Run this program only on specified platforms

40. Only When a User Is Logged On

41. Advertisement

42. True

43. False

Explanation: If the clients are located over slow links, they will not be required to run the program if the setting Assignments Are Not Mandatory Over Slow Links is enabled.

44. Greenwich Mean Time

45. True

46. False

Explanation: When the collection was created, a copy of the query was saved to the SQL server and associated with the collection. The query the collection was originally based on is a separate unrelated object.

47. False

Explanation: The Package Status does not follow packages to clients but rather to distribution points.

48. Advertised Programs Wizard

Explanation: The Advertised Programs Wizard is launched by clicking on the Advertised Programs applet in Control Panel.

49. Administrative

50. Client access points, clients who have received it.

51. True

Configuring and Using Software Metering

52. Crystal Info

53. Scheduled

54. False

Explanation: It is quite probable that an administrator might create a report and want another group or organization to be able to run it against their database. The administrator can send the report template and the recipient can use the option to set the database.

55. True

Explanation: The default Product Version Policy is set to Partial, allowing for partial version matching.

56. Metering

57. Intersite

58. 0

59. False

Explanation: Word and Excel are components within a suite, not the suite parent. In this case Microsoft Office would be the suite parent.

60. Resource Monitor

61. ANY

62. False

Explanation: Time restrictions can be restricted based on the time of day, but not day of week.

63. True

64. True

Explanation: License enforcement can be disabled by unchecking the Rules option Enforce the License Limit of This Product.

65. Excluded Programs

66. Report Wizard

Sample Test

3-1   B

Explanation: Hardware collection is enabled on a per site basis. Both 32- and 16-bit clients can participate in hardware inventory collection; however, because answers C and D use the word *only*, they are not correct.

3-2   B

Explanation: Because the administrator wants to extend the hardware properties collected for an individual client, a NOIDMIF file must be used.

3-3   B

Explanation: Because the site server will not be able to correlate the partial inventory file with a record client, it will initiate resynchronization. The current record associated with the client and its history will be deleted, and a new record will be generated. A mismatched record will not of itself corrupt the database, nor will one result in the removal of software from the originating client. Although corrupt inventory records are placed in the `Badmifs` directory, a mismatched record is not necessarily a corrupt record.

3-4   B and C

Explanation: Software and hardware inventory are independent processes with separate schedules. Clients have minimum requirements, including needing at least 3MB of virtual memory and 2MB of free space. By default, only `.exe` files are inventoried; `.com` files are ignored.

3-5   B

Explanation: The program to be executed already resides on the client, so it is not necessary to redistribute to source files. The administrator needs to create a package and specify that it doesn't contain any files in the Data Source tab. The Update button would only update the source file on distribution points; it would not force clients to run a program.

3-6   B

Explanation: The sending priority is used to establish the precedence that should be given to a package when it is being sent to a child site. The default priority is medium.

3-7   C

Explanation: You can set start times relative to Greenwich Mean Time so that clients in multiple time zones can execute advertised programs simultaneously; however, this is an option. Advertisements can be set to expire but there is no assigned default expiration time. The default priority is medium.

3-8   A and D

Explanation: SMS Installer is used to create packages and installation scripts, but it does not provide a means of distributing packages. Reference computers can run any version of Windows.

Unit 4

Study Questions

Installing and Configuring an SMS Client Computer

1. True

   Explanation: Network Discovery cycles through the possible resource addresses in IP subnets, attempting to locate resources for which it can generate DDRs.

2. False

   Explanation: The role of the discovery process is limited to identifying resources. Of itself, discovering a client or server does not force the installation of the SMS client software.

3. False

   Explanation: In general, the discovery process precedes the installation of SMS client software. Additionally, discovery can identify and enumerate resources such as routers and printers that would never be the recipients of SMS client software.

4. Domains

5. Keep Logon Point List for Discovery and Installation Synchronized

6. True

7. False

   Explanation: Windows NT clients can use `.bat`, `.cmd`, and `.exe` files as logon scripts. SMS can modify only `.bat` and `.cmd` files.

8. Smsls.bat

9. 3.11, 3.12

10. NetWare 3.*x* servers

11. False

    Explanation: Although you can configure polling settings, this is the frequency with which the site server will collect information from CAPs located on NetWare servers. The NetWare servers are passive elements in the discovery process; they do not report information.

12. Discovery Data Record (DDR)

13. System

14. False

    Explanation: NetWare NDS servers do not have a system logon script. NetWare NDS Logon Discovery modifies container logon scripts.

15. Container objects

16. True

17. Slow network

18. Windows NT Remote Client Installation

19. Browsers

20. Public

21. 0

22. Subnet

23. IP address, name

24. True

25. Heartbeat Discovery

26. False

    Explanation: Heartbeat Discovery can be scheduled to run at specific hourly, daily, or weekly intervals.

27. Windows Networking User Group Discovery

28. Windows Networking User Account Discovery

29. False

    Explanation: The SMS Control Panel applet is installed on Windows-based clients when they are discovered. It does not necessarily mean that the SMS client software has been installed.

30. True

31. Smsman.exe

32. Smsman16.exe

33. False

    Explanation: The installation process is initiated only for clients whose accounts are in the same context as containers listed as logon points.

34. MS, SMS

35. False

    Explanation: Although the applets listed in the question may be installed, the actual applets installed depends on which client agents have been enabled.

36. True

Installing and Configuring Remote Utilities on Client Computers

37. False

    Explanation: The Remote Tools Client Agent can be installed on both Windows NT and Windows 3.*x* clients.

38. False

    Explanation: Any Windows NT users and Global Groups listed in the Administrators list under the security tab can perform remote control.

39. True

40. Full, Limited, None

41. False

Explanation: The visible indicator will not be displayed if the Notification tab option Show Visible Indicator is set to Never.

42. False

Explanation: Compression can be set per site to low, high, or automatic. Deciding which setting to choose should be based on the processor types and speeds in use at a given site. Low should be used when all of the NT clients to be remote controlled have a Pentium 150MHZ or below. High should be used when all NT clients to be remote controlled have a Pentium greater than 150MHz. If you are unsure or have an environment of mixed-speed clients, you should select Automatic, to have SMS determine which level to use on a per-client basis.

43. NetBIOS Lana number

44. Windows NT, Windows 3.x

45. False

Explanation: The remote NT diagnostics program does have access to many settings, including interrupts and environment variable values; however, it provides read-only access so modifications cannot be performed. For this function, use Remote Control and go directly into Control Panel or the registry to make those changes.

46. True

47. Remote Execute

Installing and Configuring Windows NT Event to SNMP Trap Translator

48. SNMP

49. TCP/IP, SNMP

50. Public

Installing and Configuring Health Monitor to Monitor Windows NT Server Computers

51. Diskperf

52. False

Explanation: The Health Monitor Agent can only be installed on Windows NT 4–based systems. SMS site systems can include Novell NetWare Bindery and NDS-based servers, which cannot run the Health Monitor Agent.

Sample Test

4-1   A

Explanation: NetWare 3.*x* clients are validated by bindery-based servers (i.e., NetWare 3.11). Upon validation, clients are automatically passed a copy of the system login script (net$log.dat) to execute which would now call smsls.bat. If you wanted to enable NetWare Bindery Server Logon Discovery or NetWare Bindery Server Logon Installation only for a few select clients, it would be necessary to modify the user login scripts manually.

4-2   C

Explanation: The hop count is used to control the range that will be spanned by the Network Discovery process. The hop count defaults to zero, which means that only resources on the local subnet will be discovered. To discover all subnets, the hop count should be set to the number of routers that need to be crossed to reach the outermost subnet. Network Trace uses information gathered by Network Discovery but does not actually discover information on its own. Heartbeat Discovery is used to verify the existence of previously discovered resources.

4-3 D

Explanation: It is not necessary to enable any form of Discovery Process to discover site systems as resources. This is managed automatically by SMS using the Server Discovery method. You can not configure nor disable Server Discovery.

4-4 A, B, and E

Explanation: You can bind any one of the following protocols to the Remote Tools Client Agent: NetBEUI, TCP/IP, or IPX. The DLC protocol is generally used with network printers and SNA gateways or older HP printers. Macintosh clients cannot be remote controlled, so AppleTalk would not function with the agent.

4-5 C or D

Explanation: Reconfiguring the network would be not only tedious and inefficient but also impossible to perform on a per-group basis for users who are members of multiple groups. Placing the NT groups in NDS containers is also not possible. Either option C or D will work; however, option C does not force the client to install the software but only informs them of its existence.

4-6 D

Explanation: Heartbeat Discovery is used to periodically poll resources that have already been discovered. This is especially useful for systems that do not have anyone logged on locally, such as a SQL server. Option A does not exist, although Windows NT Remote Client Installation does.

4-7 A

Explanation: The client communicates with the SMS site systems using client access points as intermediary drop-off and pick-up points. The DDR information is retrieved and passed to the SQL server by the Discovery Data Manager.

4-8 B and D

Explanation: The Remote Tools Client Agent can run on both Windows NT and Windows 3.*x* clients. Although there are multiple protocols to choose from, only a single protocol can be bound to the agent at a given time. Any users or groups who are listed under Administrators on the Security tab can remote control NT clients.

4-9   All

Explanation: The Event to Trap Translator relies on the SNMP agent to forward traps to an SNMP manager. The events for which to generate traps are defined by Event Source and Event ID as listed in the NT Event Log.

4-10   D

Explanation: A single resource can be included in multiple SMS sites. For example, if two sites include overlapping subnets in their boundaries, it is possible for resources in those subnets to appear as resources in both sites and potentially become a client in both sites. It is not necessary to define sites prior to resource discovery. Although an IP address is a requirement of Network Discovery, this is not a limitation imposed by other forms of discovery. Routers and printers with IP addresses can be discovered using Network Discovery.

Unit 5

Study Questions

Identifying Changes to a Site Server after SMS Installation

1. `HKEY_LOCAL_MACHINE\SOFTWARE\Microsoft\SMS`

2. `HKEY_LOCAL_MACHINE\CurrentControlSet\Services`

3. NT

4. Service Manager

Monitoring SMS Status Messages

5. NT Event Log

6. Thresholds

7. Status Reporting

8. False

   Explanation: You can control the settings only for advertisements, site systems, and components.

9. False

   Explanation: Status Filter Rules and Status Summarizer properties determine if messages should be passed to parent sites.

10. Informational, warning, error

11. Status Filter Rules

12. False

13. 100K

14. 1MB

15. Inhinv32.log

16. Sinv32.log

17. cqmgr32.log

Monitoring the Progress of SMS Processes

18. Client Component Configuration Manager (CCIM)

19. True

20. 15

21. Hinv32.log

22. Sms_def.mof

23. `.hic`

24. `.hid`

25. Inbox

26. GSNW, IntraNetWare Client

27. `Insinv32.log`

28. 30

29. `.sic`

30. Distribution Manager

31. `Sender.log`

32. True

33. Security

34. Permitted Viewers

35. `Liccli.log`

36. Excluded

37. Application

38. Status Message

Using SMS Utilities to Monitor SMS Functions

39. Promiscuous

40. Experts

41. Average Server Response Time, Top Users, and Protocol Distribution

42. Network Monitor Control Tool

43. False

44. Network Trace

45. Tracert

Optimizing SQL Server for SMS

46. False

47. Tempdb

Optimizing Sender Network Utilization

48. True

Explanation: You may want to increase the maximum concurrent sendings per site for a given sender when you have significant available bandwidth. This increases the sender's capacity for data transfer but at the expense of available bandwidth.

Monitoring the SMS Database

49. SQL dump or backup

50. 90

51. Update Statistics

Backing Up an SMS Site

52. False

53. False

54. Registry

Sample Test

5-1   B

Explanation: Status Filter Rules can be created to take an action when a message is encountered from a particular component, of a certain severity, with a certain ID, and so on. One of the action options is to not forward the message to the parent site.

5-2   A

Explanation: The Network Discovery log is not enabled by default. To turn the logging on, you must run the SMS Service Manager. If a log file exceeds its maximum size, it will simply roll over but will not be deleted or renamed.

5-3   B

Explanation: SMS Trace is included with SMS 2 in the RESKIT subdirectory. While viewing log files with SMS Trace, new entries are shown, along with historical information. TRACER only shows new information being added and cannot support multiple files. Neither the SMS Administrator Console nor MOF Manager provides a way to view log files.

5-4   B and C

Explanation: Because NetWare 3.12 is a bindery-based system, GSNW and NWLink must be installed on the site server in order to connect. The IntraNetWare client would be required for Novell Directory Services (NDS)–based NetWare servers (e.g., 4.11).

5-5   D

Explanation: Clients report hardware and software inventory to all sites of which they are members. If a client is a member of multiple sites, they maintain the schedule for agents based upon the site that they installed the agent from. Only if all of a client's sites disable an agent will the agent be removed from the client.

5-6   A

Explanation: Only those listed in the Permitted Viewers list can remote control systems. The SMS Admins group is used to specify who can connect to the site database but has nothing to do with remote control. The required minimum link is 28.8kbps. The fact that access is being denied shows the systems have a common protocol. It is not necessary to be validated by a domain controller to perform remote control.

5-7 C

Explanation: The most effective tool to use would be the Network Monitor Control Tool. This tool monitors the network in real-time for a variety of conditions, including the presence of rogue DHCP servers.

5-8 D

Explanation: Network Trace uses the tracert command to draw a graphical map showing the relationship between site systems. The roles that each site system plays are displayed.

5-9 A and B

Explanation: Rebuilding the indexes reduces the amount of physical overhead in the database. Updating the statistics refreshes the information in the distribution pages used by the SQL query optimizer, when determining which indexes, if any, to use when executing a given query.

5-10 A, B, and C

Explanation: To restore the SQL database properly to the same processor, sort order, and character set should be used. The security mode can be changed without affecting the data itself. The security mode can be specified when the SMS site is reset.

5-11 D

Explanation: The transaction log can be backed up separately from the database (incremental backup) only when the data and log are on separate devices. Additionally, if the option to Truncate Logon Checkpoint is turned on, only full backups can be performed.

Unit 6

Study Questions

Choosing the Appropriate Diagnostic Tool

1. Network Monitor

   2. Network Monitor Control Tool

   3. Dumpsend

   4. WBEMtest

   5. SMS Trace

   6. Status Message Viewer

Diagnosing and Resolving SMS Site System Installation Problems

   7. `Smssetup.log`

   8. NTFS, 1GB

   9. Five

   10. Domain Admins

   11. False

   Explanation: The partition must be already be in NTFS format before installation.

   12. `Cqmgr32.log`

   13. False

   Explanation: All controllers in specified domains are made CAPs when logon installation or discovery is enabled.

Diagnosing and Resolving Client Installation Problems

   14. 14MB

   15. False

   Explanation: When a system is not within the site boundaries (assigned), it is not possible for it to become a client.

Diagnosing and Resolving Software Distribution Problems

16. IntraNetWare

Explanation: The IntraNetWare client lets the server connect to the NDS-based system.

17. GSNW

Explanation: Installing GSNW on the site server lets it connect to the bindery-based Novell 3.*x* server.

18. Distribution Manager

Diagnosing and Resolving Inventory Collection Problems

19. `Inhinv32.log`

20. False

Explanation: The site from which the agent was installed provides the initial schedule; however, if a site listed higher in the client's configuration list later enables the agent with a different schedule the new one will be used.

21. True

Diagnosing and Resolving Remote Control Problems

22. False

Explanation: The SMS Admins members receive the right to connect to the SMS provider. The SMS Admins group is a local group and is not included in the Permitted Viewers list.

23. False

Explanation: The Permitted Viewers list is centrally controlled by the SMS site administrator. The entries are then copied to the clients' registries. It is not recommended, however, to update the list directly on each client.

24. One

25. WINS, LMHOSTS

26. True

Diagnosing and Resolving Software Metering Problems

27. False

Explanation: Although licensing is not enforced when a client cannot contact a license server, their usage will be reported when they reconnect.

28. False

Explanation: Only 32-bit Windows-based clients support software metering. This includes Windows 95/98 and Windows NT clients.

29. 4

30. Header

31. `Liccli.log`

Diagnosing and Resolving SNMP Integration Problems

32. True

33. False

Explanation: The trap destination must be an actual SNMP manager. A third-party product could be loaded on the primary site server, but one is not provided.

34. Windows NT

35. True

Explanation: It is necessary for the Windows NT SNMP agent to be preinstalled and configured before you install the SNMP Event to Trap Translator agent.

Restoring an SMS Site

36. False

Explanation: The new SQL server does not have to have the same machine name, but it does require the same processor type, sort order, and character set as the original SQL server. The SMS primary site server can be updated with the new SQL server information by resetting the site using SMS Setup.

37. True

38. Sitectrl.ct0

39. True

40. True

41. True

Diagnosing and Resolving Site-to-Site Communication Problems

42. Time, Priority

Explanation: The scheduler determines the proper sender to use when sending to an address based on the time of day and the priority of data. If a preferred sender was specified for a package, it will be used if available. Bandwidth restrictions can be entered in address properties, but this is not a determining factor in whether or not to use a particular sender.

43. SMS Service Manager

44. Sender.log

Sample Test

6-1 B

Explanation: The Network Monitor Control Tool can identify the use of unauthorized Network Monitors. Although Software Metering Manager would effectively prevent in-house machines from running Network Monitor, it would require visitors' machines to be installed as SMS clients.

6-2   B

Explanation: Regardless of where the SMS service account is located, by default, only the domain containing the primary site server is entered by default in the list of logon points.

6-3   A, B, and D

Explanation: The hard disk space requirements for a secondary site server differ from those of a primary site server. All requirements are basically the same except that a secondary site server requires a minimum of only 500MB versus the 1GB required by the primary site server.

6-4   D

Explanation: The administrator should have installed the IntraNetWare client instead of GSNW, because the target server is using NDS. NetWare volumes cannot be formatted with NTFS, but this is not required as NetWare has its own security mechanisms. DPs must be created on NetWare servers for clients that can only connect to Novell servers to be able to install packages. Even if the server were bindery-based (3.x) it would not be necessary to start the GSNW service; only the client portion is use.

6-5   D

Explanation: Windows for Workgroup clients cannot run the software metering agent and therefore cannot create a liccli.log file. The default maximum client log file size is 100KB. The default maximum collected file size is set to 1MB. If permissions on the CAP had been changed, this could result in a problem; however, it is not the most probable answer.

6-6   B

Explanation: The SNMP Event to Trap Translator agent is performing its job properly and does not need to be reinstalled. The domain name assigned to the site server is unrelated to the SNMP community name. WINS server installation is not a requirement for SNMP. The Windows NT SNMP agent is responsible for sending the trap messages to the proper location. Simply modify the trap destination address in the Windows NT SNMP agent service settings.

6-7   A

Explanation: By default, the remote control agent will be bound to the TCP/IP on Windows NT–based systems. If the clients were not all Windows NT–based, then those that were not would bind the agent to the first installed protocol. Although the agent can be installed on clients with multiple protocols, it will bind only to a single protocol. Because all clients, in this scenario, have the agent bound to TCP/IP, the administrator's computer would require only TCP/IP.

6-8   B or D

Explanation: Real-time license verification must be enabled because the `liccli.log` file is recording the granting of licenses to clients. If products were excluded, clients would not need to request licenses for them. The answer is either that enforcement of license limits is not specified for any products, or that license limits will not be enforced until after a trend is established. You should generally establish a trend before enforcing license limits, so that the system can properly balance licenses without causing users to be denied access to applications unnecessarily. After a trend has been established, and license balancing has occurred, you can then remove the condition from the registered product to initiate license-limit enforcement.

Unit 7

Final Exam

7-1   A, B, and D

Explanation: The use of the Express Setup method causes all installation and discovery methods, with the exception of Network Discovery, to be enabled. Enabling either Windows NT Logon Discovery or Windows NT Logon Installation will result in SMSLOGON share points being created on all controllers of which the site server is a member. Member servers, even if being used as site servers, cannot validate logons; therefore, they do not receive SMSLOGON points. Finally, although using Express Setup does enable both the Windows NT Logon Discovery and Windows NT Logon Installation methods, it does not automatically elect to configure logon scripts.

7-2   C

Explanation: A unique three-character site code must be defined during the installation for each site in an SMS hierarchy, regardless of its position in the hierarchy. The site code cannot be modified after installation.

7-3   D

Explanation: When calculating the required number of SQL User Connections, you must allow five connections for each concurrent connection via the SMS Administrator Console, or 50 base connections for services, plus any connections required for other SQL applications accessing the same SQL Server.

The number of configured connections can be changed using either the SQL Enterprise Manager or the `SP_CONFIGURE` stored procedure.

7-4   C

Explanation: SMS 1.2 and SMS 2 sites can be included in the same hierarchy; however, SMS 2 sites cannot be child sites of SMS 1.2 sites under any circumstances.

7-5   A, C, and D

Explanation: An SMS 1.2 to 2 site upgrade can be initiated either locally or from its parent site. Because SMS 2 sites cannot report to SMS 1.2 sites, the topmost site in the hierarchy has to be upgraded first. Secondary sites must be reinstalled in order become primary sites.

7-6   D

Explanation: When attempting to administer a secondary site, it is necessary to connect to its parent site's database. In the scenario, the administrator's mistake is entering the name of the secondary site server.

7-7   A, B, and D

Explanation: Because all of the various senders, except the courier, run as threads of SMS Executive, senders can only reside on Windows NT servers. The courier sender does not require configuration, as it does not actively monitor data transmission. Sites can use multiple senders of the same type; however, only one sender of each type is allowed per server. The SMS_SITE share corresponds to the `Sms\Inboxes\Despoolr.box\Receive` folder, which is used as the entry point for data to the site.

7-8   A, B, D, and E

Explanation: Logon servers are used in conjunction with various methods of logon discovery and installation. Because Windows NT member servers don't validate logons, they cannot be used in this role.

7-9   A

Explanation: Client access points (CAPs) are the primary points of communication between SMS clients and servers. Although CAPs are initially located on the primary site server, it may be advantageous later to add a CAP to another site system and remove the CAP role from the primary site server entirely. This is done in order to limit the number of clients communicating directly with share points located on the primary site server. This in turn increases the availability of local resources for SMS services.

7-10   C and D

Explanation: Secondary sites cannot be simply detached and reattached, like primary sites. The parent of a secondary site is determined during its installation, so the only way to change that parent is by uninstalling and reinstalling the secondary site.

7-11   B

Explanation: Traveling mode can be enabled by selecting the option **This computer connects to the network from different locations**, in the SMS applet. Using a static IP address would not make any difference, and these discovery and installation methods do not determine assignment.

7-12   D

Explanation: Heartbeat Discovery ensures that Discovery Data Records are updated for all systems, including those where no one regularly logs on. By default, this occurs on a weekly basis. Also by default, the database maintenance task to delete aged discovery data removes records that are not updated within the last 3 months.

7-13   B, C, and D

Explanation: NetWare servers cannot run the SMS Executive; an NLM version does not exist. NetWare servers can act as site systems. Their volumes can be used as both CAPs and DPs. Because the site server must initiate contact with the NetWare servers, it is necessary for the site server to be a NetWare Client.

7-14 A

Explanation: NetWare-based systems are incapable of running the SMS Executive, and hence the Inbox Manager Assistant. Therefore, the Inbox Manager periodically polls the NetWare-based CAPs to retrieve information.

7-15 A

Explanation: MOF Manager provides the simplest means of editing the SMS_DEF.MOF. Since MOF files are text files, it would be possible to edit the file in Word; however, it is more complicated. The SMS Administrator Console does not provide a means of editing the file. `Hinv32.exe` is the filename of the 32-bit Hardware Inventory Agent.

7-16 B

Explanation: `Hinv32.log` is the log file that corresponds with the Hardware Inventory Agent on the client. The `Inhinv32.log` details the Hardware Inventory Agent installation. The `Inventry.log` is fictitious. The `Cqmgr32.log` relates to the activities of the Copy Queue Manager.

7-17 D

Explanation: By default, only files with an extension of .exe are inventoried.

7-18 D

Explanation: User and Group discovery is supported only for Windows NT users and groups. Both user and group discovery is configured separately to poll the primary domain controller of selected domains at given intervals.

7-19 E

Explanation: Collectively, answers A through D add up to a partial solution, but they would prove ineffective and cumbersome. By enforcing the permitted times that the game would be available via the Software Metering Agent their ability to access the file from the server would not be relevant.

It would of course be best to meter the software based upon the header information, otherwise it would be possible for them to simply rename the game and execute it.

7-20 B

Explanation: By excluding the applications in the Software Metering Console, they will simply be ignored by the clients. There will be no record of their having been executed.

7-21 C and D

Explanation: Callback priority is set on a per user basis. When a user requests to be notified when a license becomes available, the request lives for 30 minutes. Because software metering is not supported for NetWare clients, they would never receive callback notifications. Software metering is supported only on Windows NT or Windows 95 client machines where the user logs on to a domain.

7-22 B

Explanation: Remote control is designed to work effectively across a 28.8kbps link.

7-23 C

Explanation: Remote control is supported for both 16-bit and 32-bit Windows clients. Any valid user or group can be made a member of the Permitted Viewers list. Remote Control sessions are logged in the NT Security Event Log. While clients with 150MHz processors are capable of high-compression it is not a requirement for remote control.

7-24 D

Explanation: The database option Truncate Log On Checkpoint is used automatically to remove committed transactions from the transaction log. When this option is enabled, only full backups of the database can be performed.

7-25 B

Explanation: Collection definitions passed from parent sites to child sites cannot be modified at the child site.

7-26 D

7-27 A, B, C, and D

Explanation: Enabling the task Backup the Site Server results in a backup of all pertinent SMS data to a directory you specify on the site server.

Since the backup creates a copy of the data on the hard disk, it is not in itself a substitute for a true backup to tape. Unlike the option to Export the SMS Database, it is not necessary to create a SQL backup device but rather only to specify a directory.

7-28   A, B, and C

Explanation: When restoring a backup of a primary site server to a new computer, it must have the same processor type, domain name, machine name, and SMS installation drive and directory. The IP address will not affect the operation of the site system.

7-29   A

Explanation: When SMS is first installed, the SMS Admins group is created as a local group on the system housing the SMS Provider. Member-ship in this group allows sufficient privileges within WBEM security to connect to the SQL Server. Technically, it would be possible to use `WBEMperm.exe` and set permissions for the user directly, but this is beyond the scope of the exam.

7-30   C and D

Explanation: SMS class and instance security settings cannot be explicitly denied. Because the desired goal is to allow all systems except the accounting systems to have remote control, it is best to use instance security settings and set the options for the collection from which accounting systems have been filtered out.

7-31   A

Explanation: Clients can install their core components either from CAPs or from logon points. DPs are used for package installation. NT clients will generate Client Configuration Requests (CCRs) asking that SMS software be pushed to them if the local user has insufficient rights. Installation is most often initiated by logon, but it can be initiated manually or even automatically when NT clients are discovered.

7-32   C and D

Explanation: Clients can be assigned to multiple sites, but their primary site will control many of their agent settings. Clients that are not assigned can be discovered, as in the case of a domain that spans multiple subnets or when using Network Discovery. Clients compare their IP subnet or IPX network number to the site boundaries (`netconf.ncf`) list retrieved from a CAP in order to determine assignment.

7-33   A, C, and D

Explanation: Express Setup enables all installation and discovery methods, except Network Discovery. Running the express setup alone will result in the creation of SMS logon points on all controllers in DomainX. Member servers don't validate logons, so they're never used as SMS logon points. You can configure logon scripts for Windows

NT Logon Discovery or Windows NT Logon Installation by setting the option to automatically configure logon scripts. Although discovery and installation are independent processes, both discovery and installation were enabled in the scenario because Express Setup was used.

7-34 A, B, and D

Explanation: If a client finds that it is not assigned, it will terminate installation of SMS client software. Clients use `slownet.exe` to determine their connection speed; if it is less than 40kbps (configurable), the client will not be installed. Although NTFS is a requirement of site servers, it is not a requirement of clients. Clients will require between 14MB and 20MB of free disk space, depending on which agents have been enabled.

7-35 A

Explanation: After installing the Hardware Inventory Agent, there is a 15-minute delay before its initiation. For the Software Inventory Agent the delay is 30 minutes. Time synchronization with the site server is more of an issue when advertisements are involved. If the SQL Server were down, it would not be possible to connect to the site database to view any information. The client computer does not require a reboot to activate the agents.

7-36 D

Explanation: Although either the Hardware Inventory Agent being disabled or the IDMIF being corrupt could result in data not being reported, the administrator is probably looking in the wrong place. IDMIF files are used to create entirely new classes of objects, and do not simply contain attributes, as is the case with NOIDMIFs. Resource Explorer does not reflect the new classes, so the administrator must write a custom query to view the collected data.

7-37 B, C, and D

Explanation: Because the execution of the program must occur simultaneously throughout the organization, it is necessary to base the execution on Greenwich Mean Time. Because EST is GMT plus 5, the time must be adjusted to compensate. Also, it would be necessary to make the assignment mandatory to ensure that it is executed properly.

7-38 A

Explanation: When collections are based on a query, the query definition is saved with the collection. From that point on, the query originally used to define the collection is independent of the one used when the collection is updated. The collection can be updated on a schedule, forcing the collection's query to be executed periodically. Remember that refreshing the view in the SMS Administrator Console does not update the collections.

7-39   A and B

Explanation: Because the package was created using a package definition file, it will realistically contain the proper program settings, including which operating systems and platforms are supported. The check of the requirements is transparent to the user. Machines that don't meet the requirements simply don't run or display the advertised program.

7-40   D

Explanation: Answers A through C would all work well together if each remote location were a separate site. With SMS 2, you can't schedule the time when distribution will occur to DPs in the originating site.

7-41   A, B, or C

Explanation: The most common cause for failure of an advertisement to appear is the times not being properly synchronized. The client may well receive the advertisement but may believe it is not yet time to show it to the user. If a client system does not meet the advertisement's operating system or platform requirements, the advertisement will not be displayed. Inadequate permissions will prevent the program from properly executing but not from displaying.

7-42   B, C, and D

Explanation: The fact that the administrator was receiving data on which to report shows that the agent was installed and enabled. If the client agent is not configured to force real-time license verification, less traffic is generated, but the client will never be denied, regardless of license availability. You can elect not to enforce license limits or not to enforce them until a trend is determined.

7-43   A, C, and D

Explanation: Health Monitor depends on the Performance Monitor counters to determine whether an application is performing within certain thresholds. Health Monitor is perhaps the utility of choice here, but you could also configure the Alert View in Performance Monitor to take an action or provide notification. The SNMP Event to Trap

Translator could provide notification, but the stopping of the server would need to be reported to the NT Event Log and the administrator would require a trap monitor.

7-44 A

Explanation: The minimum operating system for a reference computer is Windows 3.*x*. The reference computer should not be an SMS server or SMS client since these result in unwanted activity on the system while packages are being built.

7-45 A, C, and D

Explanation: When the scheduler is determining which sender to use, it checks the availability of a sender for the time of day and priority. Once a sender is selected, the traffic can be limited to a percentage of the available bandwidth. The bandwidth setting is configured at the address, not at the sender. It is not possible to set restrictions based on collection name.

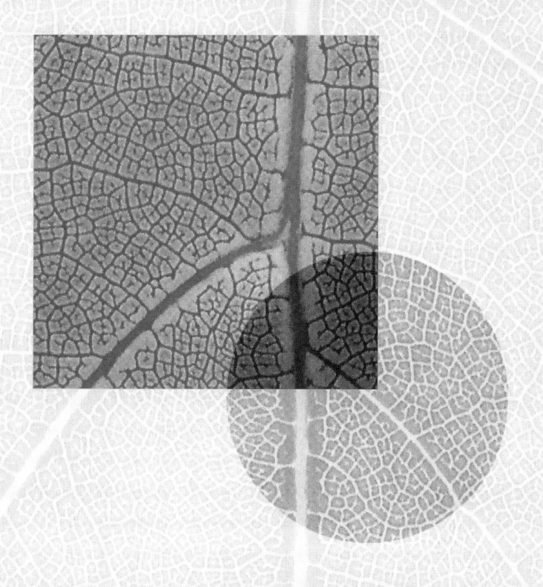

Glossary

A

Access account   This account is one to which a user or group of users is tied so that they can access a package on a distribution point. In this way, only those people who are in a group that the access account is using can run certain advertised programs from the distribution point.

Address   A unique identifier of some kind that serves to identify a computer or piece of network gear on a network. It can be a MAC address, IP address, or IPX network number. SMS uses addresses to connect site systems together and its senders use addresses to send information to other sites.

Advertise   To go through the activity of making a program available to the members of a collection or collections.

Advertised program   An advertised program is one that has been advertised to a collection, but one in which the members of the collection are not required to run it.

Advertised Programs Manager (APM)   An SMS package can be given the ability to generate a Status MIF file that reports the progress of installation back to the site server. In SMS 2, the Advertised Programs Manager converts these Status MIF messages into SMS Status messages and routes them back to the site server.

Advertisement   A notification to members of certain collections that a program is available for them to run.

Alert   An audible or visual error or warning to an administrator notifying her of a potential problem. The administrator will see these alerts on-screen in the form of an alert box. Textual information within these alert boxes can be very verbose, giving pretty in-depth information. Software metering is one SMS component that can be configured to make heavy use of alerts.

Aliasing   This is a technique used in software metering. You have one executable that you're tracking within software metering and you have another very similar to it that you want to also consider akin to the executable already being tracked. For example, suppose that, for some reason, you wanted to track smsman.exe and smsman16.exe (not that you ever would, of course—this is just an example). One `.exe` is 32-bit (`smsman.exe`) while the other is 16-bit. But they do essentially the same job. You would set software metering up so that it tracked all occurrences of `smsman.exe` as, say, "SMS Manual Client Installation Software," and then you'd alias `smsman16.exe` to be tracked in the same way. This way, whenever either program was used on a computer, it would account for one license of "SMS Manual Client Installation Software."

Assigned program   An assigned program is mandatory and must be run by members of the collection(s) the program is targeted for. The administrator can configure the program so that it may be run one or more times. He can also set it up so that the user receiving the program can opt to run the program immediately, at any time between now and the time the program runs, or automatically when the program runs.

Assigning   When an administrator sets up and sends out a mandatory program to members of a collection, she is said to be *assigning* that program.

Asynchronous RAS sender   One of the SMS communications senders. This one uses standard telephone lines (asynchronous lines) and Windows NT RAS to communicate with other SMS sites.

Attribute class   An object type is comprised of a set of attributes that represents some object in the SMS database—a client or a package could be examples of this. An attribute class is a container-type object that groups these attributes into an object type. *Computer system* is an example of an attribute class. A specific set of attributes make up a given computer system object type.

B

BackOffice   Microsoft's line of client/server support applications that run on Windows NT Server. Some components of BackOffice include Microsoft SQL Server, Systems Management Server (SMS), Internet Information Server (IIS), Exchange Server, SNA Server, Site Server, FrontPage 2000, and Proxy Server.

Backup device   A file or tape to which SQL Server backs up a database. Also called a *dump device*. SQL has no built-in backup devices that point to files or tapes. You will need to create all of your backup devices that point to files or tapes, or utilize third-party tape backup software with SQL Server modules that allow you to backup your SQL databases to tape.

Backup domain controller (BDC)   A server that keeps a copy of the authentication database from the Primary Domain Controller (PDC). Users can log in to either the PDC or to any of the BDCs.

Boundary(ies)   The IP subnet(s) and/or IPX network number(s) that the SMS site uses for all of its operations. By default, the subnet that the site server was installed in becomes the first boundary, but you can edit the site's properties and add others. You can have both IP subnets and IPX network numbers as part of the same site boundary.

Broadcast   A signal that is sent to all nodes on the network, including computers and intelligent network gear.

Browser   See *Web browser*.

Buffer   A part of a computer system's memory that is reserved as a temporary holding place for data until it moves on to its final destination. For example, data waiting to be printed is buffered to memory until the printer is freed up and ready to accept the printout.

C

Callback   This is a very interesting feature of software metering. When a user tries to obtain a software license, but none is available, he is presented with a callback screen. At that time he can choose to be notified when a license has freed up or he can elect to not pursue a license at that time. If he elects to be notified, when a license becomes available, he is notified by SMS of this fact and obtains the license for a (configurable) amount of time.

CAP   See *Client Access Point*.

Capture   The act of using Network Monitor to receive all frames from the network, recording frames of a particular type for review, and then storing the desired frames in a buffer.

Capture file   Frames that are captured and stored to a .cap file for later Network Monitor review are called *capture files*.

Capture filter   In Network Monitor: a method of rooting out undesired frames and capturing only those of a desired type. The desired frames are captured to a temporary file.

Captured data   As per the above definition, any captured frames that meet a certain filter criteria are called *captured data*.

Central site   A central site is the highest primary site in the SMS hierarchy. Some companies may have two parallel SMS hierarchies, in which case there wouldn't be an overall central site, but two or more parallel central sites.

Child site   An SMS hierarchy term, a child site is an SMS site that reports to a parent SMS site. The central site server is not a child but can be a parent to many child sites. Child sites that are comprised of primary site servers can be parents of other child sites.

CIMOM   See *Common Information Model Object Manager*.

Client   A computer on a network that subscribes to the services provided by SMS.

Client Access Point (CAP)   This is the main connecting point between client computers and the SMS site server. Computers get client software from CAPs. Site management information is obtained from the CAP servers. Clients deliver their inventory, collected files, and status information to CAPs.

Client agents   Software that needs to run on a client to perform a specific task is called a *client agent*.

Client components   These are the SMS applications, threads, and services that run on client computer in order to provide the client with SMS functionality. Varies according to OS type.

Client installation methods   The methods by which SMS client software can be installed on a client computer.

Client/server   A network architecture that dedicates certain computers called *servers* to act as service providers to computers called *clients*, which users operate to perform work. Servers can be dedicated to providing one or more network services, such as file storage, shared printing, communications, e-mail service, and Web response.

Client/server application   An application that is split into two components: computer-intensive processes that run on application servers and user interfaces that run on clients. Client/server applications communicate over a network.

Collected files   Administrators can collect certain files from client computers. When they're collected, they're stored on the site server. (They are not deleted from the client computer, instead a copy is obtained for the site server.)

Collection   A group of computers or resources that fit a set of membership rules. The All Windows 95 Computers collection would be an example.

Collection limiting   Writing a query in such a way that its scope is restricted to members of a specific collection.

Common Information Model (CIM)   A common data model developed by the Distribution Management Task Force (DMTF) that describes a schema and a specification for maintaining network and enterprise management information. See `www.dmtf.org` for a CIM tutorial that you can download. This is a richer inventory management format than was previously used. One of its features allows the option to pick which entries can remain static and which dynamic, permitting the administrator to choose what data is important.

Common Information Model Object Manager (CIMOM)   This is the primary component in the WBEM model. CIMOM comprises the main data repository.

Community   Devices that communicate with one another must know the community name (and sometimes password) to access the device for specific information. The typical default community is *public*. Communities are a security relationship that two SNMP devices can enter into utilizing the community name.

Complete inventory   A complete inventory is one in which all hardware or software is inventoried on a client computer. Any other time the change or *delta* between what SMS says the client has and what has changed on the computer is sent to the site server. If the inventory data has become corrupted, deleted, or if the client changes sites, then a *resynchronization* is called for and a new complete inventory is taken.

Component server   A server running one or more of the SMS components (a specific sender, for example) in order to augment the site server's processing or offload it.

Computer name   A 1- to 15-character NetBIOS name used to uniquely identify a computer on the network.

Concurrent licensing   A software metering term, this means that all users using a software product must be simultaneously licensed for it at one time.

Console tree   A hierarchical arrangement of the objects within the SMS site. You can view the console tree from the SMS Administrator console, which utilizes the MMC format. You can expand or minimize different aspects of the console tree for varied viewing.

Courier sender   A communications sender that utilizes some sort of high capacity removable media (such as a Jaz drive) that is taken out of one site server and sent to another.

Crystal Info   The reporting software that comes with SMS 2. Crystal Info is installed by default with Express setup but you have to select it in Custom setup.

D

Database   A database is composed of one or more tables (among other SQL constructs). Since Microsoft SQL Server 6.5 (with SP5) or 7 is used to keep the information about the SMS site, we call it the site database. The SMS database has several dozen tables. See *SMS site database*.

Data collection   A software metering term. It describes the movement of software usage data from the software metering server to the site server, from the child site to the parent site, or both.

Data summarization   Another software metering term, this describes the process of boiling lots of software usage down to one generalized record, thus compressing the amount of data utilized in the software metering database.

Database Consistency Checker (DBCC) SQL Server commands used to check the consistency of databases. These commands are mostly used to gather information about the status of a database, and not generally to make changes to a database.

Database device A file that stores one or more SQL Server databases. When databases are created, they can be assigned space on one or more devices.

Database management system (DBMS) An environment specifically created for the purpose of working with databases. It usually refers to an electronic system or a computer program designed to work with databases. Microsoft Access and FoxPro are both examples of database management systems.

Database Maintenance Plan Wizard A wizard provided with SQL Server 6.5 and 7 that helps you schedule backups and perform optimizations and consistency checking.

Database owner (DBO) In SQL Server, a user who has full permissions in a particular database. This includes the ability to back up and restore the database and transaction log. The SA is also considered the DBO of every database. The DBO is specified through the SP_ChangeDBOwner stored procedure.

Database object owner (DBOO) In SQL Server, a user who creates a particular database object. The DBOO has all rights on that object, including the right to allow others to use the object.

Database user See *User*.

DB-Library A set of functions and connectivity programs that allow clients to communicate with database engines.

DDR See *Discovery Data Record*.

Delta inventory When talking about a hardware or software inventory cycle, this term implies that a complete inventory has already been taken. The difference between what the existing complete inventory says it has and what has changed is called the *delta* and is sent to the site server. It's a method of reducing the amount of network bandwidth and computing resources required to maintain client inventory and is a standard part of SMS.

Delta MIF   The Management Information Format (MIF) file that is sent to the site server containing the delta inventory information.

Denial   A software metering term, this is what the user receives when either not enough licenses exist to service a software license request or the client is not authorized to be licensed for the software. The message the user receives is configurable within the SMS Administrator console.

Destination address   The address of a computer to which data is being sent.

Details pane   The right-hand section of the SMS Administrator console that shows the details of a selected item.

Discovery data   The information that pertains to a specific resource or client. This data is sent to the site server and uploaded into the discovery database. A typical discovery record might contain the IP address, a unique SMS ID (called the *SMSUID*), and other pertinent information.

Discovery database   A database that contains DDRs collected from resources in the SMS sites. Notice that we say resources because DDRs can potentially be collected from devices on the network other than client computers.

Discovery Data Record (DDR)   The record that contains the discovery information. It is forwarded to the site server and posted to the discovery database.

Discovery methods   Ways that information about resources on a network can be discovered and the information accumulated into the discovery database. There are ten discovery methods.

Display filter   A Network Monitor term, this hides categories from view within the Frame Viewer window of Network Monitor.

Distributed Management Task Force (DMTF)   Formerly known as the "Desktop Management Task Force," this is a standards body managed by a host of technical corporations for the purpose of arriving at platform-independent open solutions for managing enterprise information. Microsoft is a board member of the DMTF and has long utilized the recommendations of the DMTF in its SMS software. You can visit www.dmtf.org for more information.

Distribution point   This is a designated site system server that contains package programs and files for clients to install. By default, the central site server is the only distribution point; you must designate others. Clients receive an advertised program from their CAP and then contact their distribution point for the files and programs necessary to install the software.

Domain   This term is defined in various ways. In Microsoft networks, a domain is an arrangement of client and server computers referenced by a specific name that shares a single security permissions database. On the Internet, a domain is a named collection of hosts and subdomains. The SMS site itself is oftentimes referred to as the *SMS domain*.

Domain controller   In Windows NT networks, a server that authenticates workstation network logon requests by comparing a username and password against account information stored in the user accounts database. A user cannot access a domain without authentication from a domain controller.

Dump device   See *Backup device*.

Dynamic backup   A type of backup that allows you to back up your SQL Server databases while they are in use. Users can stay connected to the server while a dynamic backup is in progress.

Dynamic Host Configuration Protocol (DHCP)   An industry standardized method by which devices on a network can receive TCP/IP configurations from a centralized source. In the old days you'd have to maintain a listing of TCP/IP addresses and as you set a user up with an address, you'd have to cross it off the list so you didn't use it again. As you can imagine, this became pretty overwhelming as you got into the thousands of computers. DHCP came about as a result of a Request for Comment (RFC) from the TCP/IP community and was subsequently introduced into Windows NT and NetWare networks.

Dynamic link library (DLL)   A set of modular functions that can be used by many programs simultaneously. There are hundreds of functions stored within DLLs.

E

Electronic mail (e-mail) A type of client/server application that provides a routed, stored-message service between any two user e-mail accounts. E-mail accounts are not the same as user accounts, but a one-to-one relationship usually exists between them. Because all modern computers can connect to the Internet, users can send e-mail over the Internet to any location that has telephone or wireless digital service.

Enterprise Manager See *SQL Enterprise Manager*.

Enterprise network A complex network consisting of multiple servers and multiple domains over a large geographic area.

Event Some sort of circumstance that happens which necessitates the posting of an alert to an administrator, the writing of the event to a log file, or sometimes both. The SMS Event to Trap Translator can take Windows NT events (as posted to the Event Viewer) and convert them to Simple Network Management Protocol (SNMP) traps that can be viewed within standard SNMP monitoring tools. Network Monitor can also write events and these are stored in the CIMOM. The Status Message Viewer also keeps track of events and can be configured to write the events to the NT Event Viewer application log.

Event configuration file This is the file that contains the SNMP information that was translated via the SMS Event to Trap Translator.

Event to Trap Translator An SMS process that can translate Windows NT events into SNMP traps.

Excluded programs list A software metering term, this is the list of programs that the software metering client can ignore.

Expert A Network Monitoring term. This is software tool that can analyze the capture file generated from Network Monitor and help pinpoint problem areas on the network.

F

File collection   A software inventory term, this is the process of collecting files from a client computer for storing on the site server. By default five copies of the collected file can be collected and stored.

Filter   When using Network Monitor, you can place certain restrictions on the kind of incoming packet data you'd like to see. You do this by setting up a filter. See *Capture filter* or *Display filter* for more information.

Frame   A frame, also known as a *packet*, is a base network entity that contains control.

Frame Viewer window   When viewing individual frames that were captured to a file by Network Monitor, you'd use this component of the Network Monitor window.

G

GSNW (Gateway Service for NetWare)   This service comes with Windows NT Server, although it is not installed by default. GSNW allows a Windows NT computer to be both a client to a NetWare server, and to act as a gateway to the NetWare server, allowing clients to the Windows NT server to access resources on the NetWare server as if those resources came from the NT server. GSNW also requires the IPX/SPX protocol to be installed.

H

Hardware history   When viewing a client's hardware inventory in the Resource Explorer window, you can also view the history records that have been kept for this client. This is the hardware history.

Health indicator   These are graphical icons that are used within the Site System Status Summarizer and the Component Status Summarizer to give you a quick visual reference as to the health of a particular function of the SMS operation. There are three health indicators: OK, Warning, and Critical.

Hex pane   A Network Monitor term, this is the name given to the pane of Network Monitor that shows you the hexadecimal contents of captured frames.

I

Inactivity monitoring   Another software metering term, this is when you monitor software to determine whether it's being used by anyone or not.

Installer executable file   An .exe file that is generated by SMS Installer upon compilation. You can create stand-alone .exe files that will install software on client computers without user intervention and then use the package/program/advertisement methodology to get the .exe to the client computer.

Integrated security   A SQL Server security mode in which SQL Server accepts, or trusts, the Windows NT validation of a user. The Windows NT account information is used to validate the user to SQL Server. These connections are referred to as trusted connections.

Internet Protocol (IP)   The network layer protocol upon which the Internet is based. IP provides a simple connectionless packet exchange. Other protocols, such as UDP or TCP, use IP to perform their connection-oriented or guaranteed delivery services.

Internetwork Packet eXchange (IPX)   The network protocol developed by Novell for its NetWare product. IPX is a routable protocol similar to IP but much easier to manage and with lower communication overhead. The term IPX can also refer to the family of protocols that includes the Synchronous Packet eXchange (SPX) transport layer protocol, a connection-oriented protocol that guarantees delivery in order, similar to the service provided by TCP.

Interprocess communications (IPC)   A generic term describing any manner of client/server communication protocols, specifically those operating in the session, presentation, and application layers. Interprocess communications mechanisms provide a method for the client and server to trade information.

Intranet   A privately owned network based on the TCP/IP protocol suite.

Inventory   Information that the SMS Inventory Client agents have collected and forwarded to the site server database.

IP address   A 4-byte number that uniquely identifies a computer on an IP internetwork. The ISP usually assigns the first bytes of Internet IP addresses and administers them in hierarchies. Huge organizations like the government or top-level ISPs have class A addresses, large organizations and most ISPs have class B addresses, and small companies have class C addresses In a class A address, an ISP assigns the first byte, and the owning organization assigns the remaining 3 bytes. In a class B address, the ISP assigns the first 2 bytes, and the organization assigns the remaining 2 bytes. In a class C address, the ISP assigns the first 3 bytes, and the organization assigns the remaining byte. Organizations not attached to the Internet are free to assign valid IP addresses as they please.

ISQL   A command-line utility that provides a query interface to the SQL Server. You can run Transact-SQL statements as well as stored procedures and DBCC commands from ISQL.

ISQL_w   An interactive SQL interface for Windows, also called ISQL/W. This utility allows you to run all of the same commands that the ISQL command-line utility does. It has an added advantage of being a Windows interface. This allows you to run multiple queries and view the results of multiple queries in their own separate windows.

K

kernel   The core process of a preemptive operating system, consisting of a multi-tasking scheduler and the basic security services. Depending on the operating system, other services such as virtual memory drivers may also be built into the kernel. The kernel is responsible for managing the scheduling of threads and processes.

L

LAN Adapter Number (LANA)   A way to order of the protocols installed on the computer, LANA 0–7.

License balancing   A feature used by software metering in multi-site hierarchies whereby software licenses that are not being utilized in one site can be automatically transferred to another, or whereby two software metering site systems in the same site balance their licenses between themselves.

License check-out   The software metering ability to check out licenses to software so the software is available to users for a specified time period. Useful for roving users who need the software for short terms, or for administrators needing to make sure licensing is not exceeded for a given product.

License extension   The software metering ability to license the software for multiple copies of a single license. Some software is licensed so it can be used at home and at work (the theory being that you're either at home or work but not both).

License management   The replication of software metering information to all participating software metering servers in the site.

License policy   This is a file distributed by software vendors that describes the way that their software should be licensed and the number of licenses that have been purchased. The policy should contain the program's name, its version, the time zone, and language of the program. It can contain additional information about the program, such as whether it's permissible to use it concurrently.

License profile   The license profile works the same way as the license policy with the exception that the program's name, version, time zone, and language are missing.

Local address   The network address of the computer running Network Monitor.

Local group   A group that exists in a Windows NT computer's local security database. Local groups can reside on NT Workstation or NT Server computers and can contain users or global groups. Domain controllers, of course, use local groups as well, but contextually they are a little different in the way they work. For most of our SMS discussions, we're primarily concerned with local groups on the NT Workstation or NT Server member server level.

Logical operator When writing SMS queries you can group expressions together with the logical operators AND, OR, and NOT.

Logon point This is a site system role that is filled by enabling a Logon Discovery method or Logon Client Installation method. Both Windows NT domain controllers and NetWare servers can act as logon point site systems.

M

Managed Object Format (MOF) file This is a text-based file that contains the schema information that is subsequently loaded into the Common Information Model Object Manager (CIMOM). Used for hardware inventory and discovery purposes.

Management Information Format (MIF) The standard developed by the Desktop Management Task Force (DMTF) for extracting information about systems regardless of the platform the system is on.

Management Information Format (MIF) file SMS uses MIF files to obtain updated inventory information about clients. MIF files are uploaded to the site server. You can create your own ASCII-based MIF files. MIFs used by SMS are binary in nature.

Master device The device that stores SQL Server 6.5's Master database, Model database, tempdb database, and Pubs database. The Master device has a default size of 25MB.

Master list The main list of users, user groups, and computers that is used by the software metering administrator for managing the use of software products.

Media Access Control (MAC) address See *Address*.

Media Access Control (MAC) layer A sublayer of the OSI Network layer that manages network access and collision detection.

Membership rule The description of what resources can belong to a collection. You can use a query or stipulate individual resources when developing your membership rules. Query-based membership rules are dynamic in nature, so when a new client comes into the SMS domain, it is evaluated to see if it matches the membership rules for the various collections. If it does, then it is placed in the matching collections.

Microsoft Management Console (MMC)   A standardized window for viewing and manipulating the objects in Microsoft programs. The SMS Administrator console uses the MMC format. Other applications which make use of the MMC are called *snap-ins* to the MMC.

Mixed security   A SQL Server security mode that combines the functionality of both standard and Integrated security. In Mixed security, preference is given to trusted connections, but standard security can be implemented if a trusted connection is not possible.

Monitors   A new feature of Network Monitor, these are intelligent agents that watch for specific types of frames. An example is the IP Range Monitor, which watches for invalid IP addresses. Invalid IP addresses could indicate that somebody had hacked in through the firewall from the outside (or could indicate a JetDirect card that is using its default IP address). Use the Monitor Control Tool to configure monitors.

Monitor Control Tool   The NT service that configures, starts, and stops monitors.

Multi-cast   When a packet is sent out whose destination address includes more than one address, it is a multi-cast packet. It's similar to sending one e-mail to several recipients at the same time.

Multi-processing   Using two or more processors simultaneously to perform a computing task. Depending on the operating system, processing may be done asymmetrically, wherein certain processors are assigned threads independent of the load they create, or symmetrically, wherein threads are dynamically assigned to processors according to an equitable scheduling scheme. The term usually describes a multi-processing capacity built into the computer at a hardware level (meaning the computer itself supports more than one processor). However, the concept of multi-processing can also be applied to network computing applications achieved through interprocess communication mechanisms. Client/server applications are, in fact, examples of multi-processing.

Multi-tasking   The capacity of an operating system to rapidly switch among threads of execution. Multi-tasking allows processor time to be divided among threads as if each thread ran on its own slower processor. Multi-tasking operating systems allow two or more applications to run at the same time and can provide a greater degree of service to applications than single-tasking operating systems like MS-DOS.

Multi-threaded   Multi-threaded programs have more than one chain of execution, relying on the services of a multi-tasking or multi-processing operating system to function. Multiple chains of execution allow programs to perform more than one task simultaneously. In multi-tasking computers, multi-threading is merely a convenience used to make programs run smoother and free the program from the burden of switching between tasks itself. On multi-processing computers, multi-threading allows the compute burden of the program to be spread across many processors. Programs that are not multi-threaded cannot take advantage of multiple processors in a computer.

N

Network Abstraction Layer (NAL)   A software component that hides the complexities of the network communication and operation from the client software or SMS site system component software.

NetBIOS   An applications programming interface (API) which activates network operations on PCs running under Microsoft operating systems. It is a set of network commands that the application program issues in order to transmit and receive data to another host on the network. The commands are interpreted by a network control program or network operating system that is NetBIOS-compatible. All computers on a Microsoft network have a NetBIOS name.

Network discovery   An SMS method that uses a variety of protocols—among them ARP, DHCP, OSPF, RIP, WINS, NetBIOS and SNMP—to discover resources on a network and network topology. Network discovery is used not only to discover systems but also to discover computers on the network in order to install client software.

Network Monitor   SMS comes with Network Monitor, a tool with advanced capabilities to capture, analyze, and view packets traversing your network.

Network Monitor Agent   Network Monitor Agent is a software agent that can reside on a Windows NT Workstation or Server. Using SMS Network Monitor, you can contact the agent and use it to collect network packet data, which is then passed back to you.

Network Trace   An SMS utility that allows you to trace the path through routers to your site systems. The route is then graphically diagrammed for you. A nice feature of Network Trace is that it has health monitors associated with it that can give you an idea of whether a site system is functioning or not.

Network operating system (NOS)   A computer operating system specifically designed to optimize a computer's ability to respond to service requests. Servers run network operating systems. Windows NT Server is a network operating system.

New Technology File System (NTFS)   A secure, transaction-oriented file system developed for Windows NT that incorporates the Windows NT security model for assigning permissions and shares. NTFS is optimized for hard drives larger than 500MB and requires too much overhead to be used on hard disk drives smaller than 50MB. Most SMS site systems require NTFS.

NIC (network interface card)   An adapter that fits into a computer, allowing it to communicate over the network.

Node   See *Station*.

NT Event Viewer   A Windows NT utility used to view Windows NT events and errors. The Application log records SQL Server events and errors, as well as events from other applications running under Windows NT.

Non-concurrent licensing   A software metering term, this is applied to software that is licensed for one license per computer (in other words, it cannot be used concurrently). The nice feature of this mode is that when a computer requests a license, no matter who utilizes the software on that computer, it is licensed. Thus it's a good use for walk-up and multi-use PCs. Microsoft does not support non-concurrent licensing.

O

Object type   A combination of attributes that describes an object in the SMS database. Examples of this would include clients, packages, advertisements, and user groups.

Offer Data Provider (ODP)   SMS client software that checks for the existence of advertisements that are valid for the computer, the logged-on user, or a group that the logged-on user belongs to.

Off-line metering   Typically used by clients who are not often connected to the network, this is a software metering technique wherein software usage is monitored and stored by the Software Metering Client Agent until the client connects to the network again. At that point, the data is uploaded to the software metering database.

Open Database Connectivity (ODBC)   An API set that defines a method of common database access. Client applications can be written to the ODBC API. ODBC uses a Data Source Name (DSN) to make a connection to a database and to load an appropriate ODBC driver. This driver will translate client calls made to the ODBC API into calls to the native interface of the database. The goal of ODBC is to provide interoperability between client applications and data resources.

Optimization   Any effort to reduce the workload on a hardware or software component by eliminating, obviating, or reducing the amount of work required of the component through any means. For instance, file caching is an optimization that reduces the workload of a hard disk drive.

Outbox   A directory where SMS services can put send request files. These files contain instructions for transferring data and instructions to other sites. In the SMS 2 system there is a separate outbox for each type of sender and for SMS processes.

P

Package   The files and instructions necessary to install a software application. It is considered to be an object and is first copied to the distribution point site systems, where the clients who have received an advertisement for the package can go to retrieve and install it.

Package definition file (PDF)   This is a text file that contains all the settings and switches information needed to install an application on a computer. The PDF doesn't contain the application code, but it *calls* the application's setup executable and passes in the information needed to install the application in a certain way. Many PDF files come with SMS for use in your packaging efforts. Because Adobe Acrobat files also have a .PDF extension, the new extension that is used for package definition files is .sms, though SMS will still be able to read .pdf files.

Package distribution   This is the activity that SMS goes through in order to send a package to a distribution point, share it out, and make it accessible to clients. When defining your package, the distribution points that you select in the package definition will participate in this package distribution activity.

Package routing   Even if an SMS site does not have an address for a distribution point, the SMS distribution process can still route the package. It does this by using available address data to figure out the path to the distribution point. It's also called *fan-out sending*.

Package source directory   The directory that contains the package source files.

Packet   See *frame*.

Parcel   A parcel is a Courier sender term that denotes any group of files being transferred from one site to another via Courier sender. The Courier Sender Manager creates parcels.

Parent site   A parent site is a site that has one or more sites below it.

Parser   A Network Monitor program that can break the protocols into separate entities for closer examination.

Permission   When setting up security rights for a user, permissions determine what that user has the capability of doing. Examples would include Read, Create, or Delete.

Permitted viewers   The users and user groups that can utilize remote control and remote tools on Windows NT clients.

Per-second statistics   A representation of the average amount of data reviewed by Network Monitor every second.

Per Seat License   A type of license that allows you to pay once for each seat (person) in your company, and then use any number of connections to any number of servers.

Per Server License   A type of license that allows you to pay for only a connection to a single server. You are then limited to the number of connections you have paid for.

Performance Monitor   A Windows NT utility that tracks statistics on individual data items, called *counters*. You can gather information about the performance of SQL Server and SMS through Performance Monitor.

Pragma statement   A line in a MIF or event configuration file that describes how the items in the file relate to items in the site database.

Preemptive multi-tasking   A multi-tasking implementation in which an interrupt routine in the kernel manages the scheduling of processor time among running threads. The threads themselves do not need to support multi-tasking in any way because the microprocessor will preempt the thread with an interrupt, save its state, update all thread priorities according to its scheduling algorithm, and pass control to the highest priority thread awaiting execution. Because of the preemptive nature, a thread that crashes will not affect the operation of other executing threads.

Primary domain controller (PDC)   In a Microsoft network, the domain server that contains the master copy of the security, computer, and user accounts databases, and that can authenticate workstations or users. The PDC can replicate its databases to one or more backup domain controllers (BDCs).

Primary site   A primary site requires a unique SQL database and can be a parent site, a child site, or both, depending on where it is in the hierarchy.

Process   A running program containing one or more threads. A process encapsulates the protected memory and environment for its threads.

Product suite   A software metering term, this describes a group of products that software metering views as one product, for the purposes of licenses. The Microsoft Office suite would be an example. One important impact of "suites" is they are monitored for two weeks in order to calculate a trend before enforcing license restrictions; non-suite applications are monitored for just one week.

Program   The instructions that SMS uses to carry out the installation of a package. A package can contain more than one program if need be. Programs typically have a command line executable or script file reference of some kind, and they also include any parameters, also called *switches* that might be necessary to fulfill some function of the package installation. For example, if your installation executable is setup.exe and you notice in the installation documentation that a –S provides you with a silent installation (in which the user is not prompted with any screens), you could include the command-line parameter in your program.

Promiscuous mode   No, it's not what you think. This is a Network Monitor term that describes the ability to read all of the packets passing over the network, regardless of their destination address. Thus you can capture and view all network traffic.

Prompted query   Queries that prompt the user for input information.

Property   A Network Monitor term, this is an area of a packet that denotes when a certain protocol is used. All packets using this protocol would have this area, or field, of the packet denoted as such.

Protocol   This is the set of rules that are agreed on for two computers to transfer information between themselves.

Q

Query   A query is composed of criteria that you stipulate in order to find certain information in the site database.

Query clause   The part of the query that is next to the logical operator.

Query criteria   The instructions used by the query to find the objects you're looking for.

Query expression   A comparative statement used in a query. "Where domain name *is like* 'NOMAD'" would be an example.

Query group   Grouping a set of expressions in a query together with parentheses creates a query group. Just as in mathematics, if you want a certain set of criteria to be evaluated before another, you can use parentheses to logically group your criteria, then separate them with logical operators.

Query hit count   The number of objects in the database that SMS found that match your criteria.

Query optimizer   In SQL Server, a mechanism that determines which index (or no index) will result in the lowest amount of logical I/O. This is done by evaluating the data and the restrictions that the query is requesting. With this information, the query optimizer estimates how many pages will be read for each possible scenario and chooses the scenario with the lowest estimated page I/O.

Query relational operator   The part of the query that compares one section with another. "Is like" or "is not equal to" are examples.

Query result format   This gives you the ability to define how you want the query to display (for example, what columns you want to see).

Query subclause   A series of expressions that is treated like a single expression.

R

RAID 5   A hard drive subsystem that writes files across multiple hard disks and multiple partitions in what are called *stripes*. It also keeps track of the information contained in each piece of the stripe with a parity checksum stored across the drives. A RAID 5 system provides faster disk access and fault tolerance.

Realtime   A method of saying that the computer's processing matches that of human time.

Reference computer   Also sometimes called a *baseline computer*, this is the computer that you use to create the SMS Installer programs that you create to send out via packages. You want it to match, as closely as possible, the computers your users are using.

Registered products   A software metering term, this describes the software on client computers that is being monitored by software metering. You can monitor a software product without enforcing its license limit if you so choose, thus giving you a feel for what software is out there. Alternately, you can use software metering to enforce licensing limits, or other restrictions based on time, user, or computer.

Registry   A database of settings required and maintained by Windows NT and its components. The Registry contains all the configuration information used by the computer. It is stored as a hierarchical structure and is made up of keys, hives, and value entries. You can use the Registry Editor (REGEDT32 or REGEDIT) to change these settings.

Relational database   A database composed of tables, which contain related data, and other objects such as views, stored procedures, rules, and defaults.

Relational database management system (RDBMS)   A database management system that supports true data and transactional integrity, and a server-side relational database engine. SQL Server is an RDBMS.

Remote capture   This is a Network Monitor term that describes the act of running a capture on one computer and displaying it on another.

Remote Control Agent   SMS software running on a client computer that enables an administrator to contact the computer for remote tools or remote control purposes.

Remote procedure call (RPC) A protocol that activates a function on a remote computer and brings back the results.

Remote tools Allow administrators to perform diagnostics support remotely.

Replication The act of copying software metering component information from one throughout the software metering organization.

Resource Any object that can be discovered by SMS and a DDR posted to the discovery database for that object. Examples include computers, routers, and printers.

Resource class The resources discovered in an SMS domain are broken into three categories: System Resource, meaning computers and network devices; User Group Resource, meaning Windows NT user groups; and User Account Resource, meaning user accounts found on computers running the Windows NT OS (including Workstation).

Resource explorer The SMS program used to view the software and hardware inventory discovered and collected from clients.

Resource manager You use this SMS program to add users, groups, and computers to the software metering master list.

Row In a SQL Server database, a complete set of columns within a single table that represent a single item of data.

S

SA (system administrator) The default login ID for SQL Server; the global administrator of the SQL Server system. This ID has no restrictions on what it can do within the SQL Server environment. By default, anyone who has logged in to SQL Server will be able to use the SA account unless you change this.

Schema An organizational description of a database.

Secondary site A secondary site does not own a database and can only be a child site. Secondary sites forward their inventory data to their parent site. They can never be parent sites to any other sites.

Security Accounts Manager (SAM)   The module of the Windows NT Executive that authenticates a username and password against a database of accounts, generating an access token that includes the user's permissions. Also known as the *directory database*.

Security identifier (SID)   A unique code that identifies a specific user or group to the Windows NT security system. Security identifiers contain a complete set of permissions for that user or group.

Security object   When talking about SMS 2 security, you divide it into two pieces: permissions and security objects. Permissions are given to administrators for the purposes of acting on a specific security object. There are six security objects: Advertisements, Collections, Packages, Queries, Sites, and Status.

Security right   The level of access given to SMS administrators. You first pick the security object you want to work with. Then you define the user or user groups that will receive this right. Finally, you assign the permissions you want these users to have for this right.

Sending   The act of transferring data, instructions, and programs between sites. You use a sender to send this information to other sites. Sending is also checked and acknowledged by SMS so it can recover from an interruption.

Sender   A thread component of SMS that uses some method of communications to send data between sites. The sender ensures that the connection is good, corrects errors, and closes the connection when the transmission is finished.

Send request file   The file used by the sender; it contains the instructions to connect to a site and transfer data.

Sender types   There are six senders:

Standard   Uses your existing LAN/WAN connections

Asynchronous RAS   Normal telephone line RAS

ISDN RAS   RAS over ISDN lines

SNA RAS   RAS over SNA connections

X25 RAS   RAS over X.25 WAN circuits

Courier   Sending data (parcels) via compact disk, floppies, or tapes

Server message block (SMB)   A protocol used for communicating between a server and a client.

Service   A process dedicated to implementing a specific function for other processes. Most Windows NT components are services. SQL Server is composed of two services, MSSQLSERVER, which is the main database engine, and SQLEXECUTIVE, which is the helper service. SMS is composed of many services: the Hierarchy Manager and Executive are some of the main ones.

Service component   SMS components that run as Windows NT services and can thus be started or stopped via Control Panel.

Service pack   A group of bug fixes and enhancements offered by Microsoft on a fairly regular basis. There are various service packs for different applications.

Simple Network Management Protocol (SNMP)   A standardized method that enables network devices (switches, routers, printers, etc.) to display information about themselves.

Site assignment   The process of defining the selected resources that'll be allowed in an SMS site.

Site assignment rules   This is the list of IP addresses and IPX network numbers that will make up the boundaries of the site.

Site code   A site code is a three-character alpha numeric code used to identify this site. It must be unique within the SMS hierarchy.

Site control file   SMS stores its settings in the site control file called `sitectl.ct0`. This file contains information about a variety of thing pertinent to the site, including status filters, site code information, and other pieces of data. This file is read and used by site system components and new secondary sites, among others.

Site database server   The site system role that is given to the computer hosting the SMS site database. This computer isn't necessarily the site server, although it could be. The SMS site database is a Microsoft SQL Server database.

Site hierarchy   SMS sites gathered together in a hierarchical organization with the central site server at the top and its primary and secondary parent and child sites beneath it. Primary sites can be a child or parent site or both. Secondary sites can only be child sites.

Site server When SMS is installed on a computer (i.e., SMS Setup has been run), that computer becomes a site server.

Site server domain The Windows NT domain that has the site server in it.

Site system A computer such as a Windows NT server, a NetWare volume, or a Windows NT share, that is appointed by the SMS administrator to act in some SMS functionality, called a *site system role*. Some site system roles include things like: distribution point, logon point, CAP, and so forth, though some computers cannot host some site systems. There are four site systems: NetWare Bindery volumes, NetWare NDS volumes, Windows NT servers, and Windows NT shares.

Site system role The role that a site system plays in the SMS Site.

SMS Administrator Console A Microsoft Management Console (MMC) that allows for the control and administration of SMS 2.

SMS client Computers that get inventoried by the SMS site, and can participate in remote tools functions, software distribution, or other SMS functions, are clients.

SMS site The group of SMS site systems that are included in the site boundaries.

SMS site database The Microsoft SQL Server database that contains site configuration and status information, hardware and software inventory, discovery data, etc.

SMS site server This is the server where SMS is installed. There can be more than one site server in an SMS hierarchy. The main site server is called the *central site server,* while site servers beneath it are just called *site servers* or *child site servers*. Primary site servers have an SMS database, secondary site servers do not. All inventory and other SMS information is uploaded to the central site server's database.

smsls.bat The primary script that SMS uses in logon scripts to discover and install the SMS client. SMSLS, because it is run as a logon script, is run from the domain controller that authenticated the client. It's important to note that if, within User Manager for Domains, you reference a batch file or logon script (with either the .bat or .cmd extension) that extension *must* be present in the user's profile in order to be updated for the call to smsls.bat.

smsls.scr The SMS script copied to NetWare servers that are a part of the SMS site. You can run this batch file from the system or user logon scripts, or manually as part of a batch file.

Snap-in Programs that have been written in such a way that they can be run from the MMC.

SNMP agent A software process running on an SNMP-enabled device that can send SNMP information to other entities requesting the information.

SNMP trap The result of an event, this is a notification sent by one SNMP device to another alerting the other device of the event.

SNMP Trap Manager The SMS process that can translate Windows NT events into SNMP traps.

SNMP Trap Translator See *Event to Trap Translator*.

Socket This term is found when talking about the TCP/IP protocol and when discussing PCMCIA (PC Card) services. We're interested in the TCP/IP term. It is an area of memory that can be logically addressed via programming in such a way as to identify a sender or a receiver.

Software metering database The SQL Server database that retains the information regarding software metering that was gleaned from the SMS clients. This is a *separate* database from the site database, but usually located on the same SQL Server.

Software metering server The designated site system(s) that handle the software metering role for the SMS site. The server is responsible for determining whether a particular software application has enough free licenses so that a requesting client can use one. It also collects usage information from the clients.

Software metering site The area that a single site server and one or more software metering servers covers.

Source address A Network Monitor term, this is a hexadecimal number that uniquely identifies a computer that is sending data.

SQL Enterprise Manager The main SQL Server administration program provided with SQL Server 6.5. Multiple servers can be monitored and maintained by SQL Enterprise Manager. SQL Server version 7 uses the Microsoft Management Console (MMC).

SQL Executive   A SQL Server service that can take care of automating tasks on your server. The service includes managers that can handle alerts processing, tasking, event processing, and replication. It works for local automation with the Localsystem account, but for many activities that occur over the network, it will need to be assigned a separate logon account that has administrative rights to the computer, as well as the "log on as a service" right.

SQL Server administrator   The individual usually responsible for the day-to-day administration of SQL Server databases. The administrator takes over where the programmer left off.

SQL Server Books Online   All of the books that normally ship with Microsoft SQL Server in an electronic format. SQL Server Books Online takes advantage of the original TechNet style interface, complete with a search engine for key words and phrases, bookmarks, and the ability to copy and paste from within it.

SQL Server Web Assistant   A SQL Server 6.5 utility that facilitates the creation of push Web pages. It can use the SQL Executive service to schedule the creation of the static Web pages in order to keep them more current.

SQLMaint   A SQL Server utility that can be used to create tasks that will take care of day-to-day administration of SQL Server. This includes automating backups, updating statistics, and rebuilding indexes. SQLMaint is configured by the Database Maintenance Plan Wizard.

Standard security   A SQL Server security mode in which SQL Server validates all connections to SQL Server regardless of that user's authentication to Windows NT. These connections are referred to as *standard* or *non-trusted* connections. Even in standard security mode, you can explicitly request a trusted connection to SQL Server.

Station   A term for a network interface card's (NIC) MAC address. Also called a *node*.

Status filter rule   A rule that the administrator writes to inform the Status Manager what actions to perform when a status message from an SMS component arrives. The Status Manager can be configured to write status messages to the site database, replicate upward to a parent site, and write to the NT Application event log. Several rules are enabled by default, so it's not left up to you to write them all.

Status message   Messages generated by SMS components are placed in the Status Message Viewer (SMV) section of the SMS Administrator.

Status message ID   Each unique status message has its own numeric identifier. This identifier will be repeated each time a status message of the same kind posts to the SMV.

Status message rule   SMS Administrators can configure status messages within the Status Message Viewer (SMV) in such a way so that they: write to the NT Application log, replicate to a parent site, or write to the site database. These are called message rules. You can have a status message both write to the NT Application log and replicate itself to its parent.

Status message severity   There are three levels of *severity* that a status message can come in with: Error, Warning, or Informational.

Status message threshold   The number of messages of the same kind that a particular component can generate before a status health indicator is changed from OK to Warning or from Warning to Critical. This same threshold concept also applies to disk space warnings on site servers and site systems.

Status message type   Status messages arrive stamped with one of three types:

   Audit   In order to provide an audit trail of a specific activity, such as packages.

   Detail   A message that contains specific detail about a process.

   Milestone   A message that arrives to denote a specific stage or event of an SMS process or action. For example, an SMS component starting or stopping would generate a milestone message.

Status Message Viewer (SMV)   The SMS Administrator Console window that allows you to view your status messages.

Status MIF   A Management Information Format (MIF) file containing information about the progress of a package installation on a client.

Status reporting level   This is the maximum number of status messages that the SMS client and server components can report to the Status Message Viewer (SMV). If the level is too high, the SMV or the NT Application log could be flooded with messages.

Status summary   Sort of an executive summary of the data collected by the status message system, you are given a summary of the overall behavior and health of the SMS system. Good for quick glance summaries of the health of the system.

Status Summarizer   The SMS component that creates the status summaries. Works in conjunction with the Status Manager component.

Status system   The entire SMS system for giving Administrators a status on the SMS site. Includes the status messages, status summarizers, and the Status Message Viewer as well as the Status Manager and Status Summarizer SMS components.

Storage object   Any place where SMS data can be stored. This includes Microsoft SQL Server databases, SQL Server transaction logs, Windows NT shares, and NetWare NDS volumes.

Subcollection   When distributing software via the package/program/ advertisement methodology of SMS 2, you target collections for the distribution. You can target more than one collection by making them subcollections of the target. Each collection targeted beneath your main collection is called a subcollection.

Subnet   A segment of the network separated by a routing device or switch and identified by a unique network number.

Subsite   A site in the SMS hierarchy that's beneath another site.

Suite component   A software component that is part of a family of components that can function separately or with one another. Microsoft Excel, for example, is a suite component of Microsoft Office. This term has import when discussing software metering.

Suite licensing   A software metering method of licensing a component within a suite in such a way that you can use the whole suite with one license.

Summary pane   A Network Monitor term, this is the pane within the Frame Viewer window that gives you a summary of the frames captured. The frame number, time the frame was captured, protocols that were used to send the frame, the source and destination addresses, and a description of the frame are all provided in the Summary Pane. The data contained within the frame that's highlighted in the Summary Pane is shown in the Frame Viewer window in hexadecimal and detail formats.

T

Table   In a SQL Server database, the object that contains rows and columns of data.

Target computers   Client computers that are targeted to receive an executable file that was created by the SMS Installer.

Task Manager   An NT application that manually views and closes running processes. Task Manager can also be used to view CPU and memory statistics. Press Ctrl+Alt+Del or Ctrl+Shift+Esc to launch the Task Manager.

Task   A job performed by a system, such as a backup procedure. In SQL Server 6.5, you can schedule tasks to run at regular intervals or when an alert is triggered. A task can run a Transact-SQL command, a command prompt utility, or replication procedures.

TechNet   Microsoft's monthly CD-ROM set that contains patches to existing programs, technical notes about issues (bugs), and white papers describing technologies in more detail. Most all of the information in TechNet can also be found on Microsoft's Web site.

Thread   A list of instructions running in a computer to perform a certain task. Each thread runs in the context of a process, which embodies the protected memory space and the environment of the threads. Multi-threaded processes can perform more than one task at the same time. SQL Server is a single process with many threads. Every user's connection is given a dedicated thread until the level of maximum worker threads is reached.

Thread component   When an SMS program that runs as a thread of the SMS Executive service runs, it is called a thread component. You can start and stop thread components via the SMS Service Manager within the SMS Administrator Console.

Transaction   In the SMS status message system, a transaction is when related status messages are grouped together as a single unit.

Transact-SQL (T-SQL)   SQL is a database language originally designed by IBM that can not only be used for queries, but can also be used to build databases and manage security of the database engine. Microsoft SQL Server uses Transact-SQL, an enhanced version of the SQL language, as its native database language.

Transaction log   In SQL Server, a reserved area in the database that stores all changes made to the database. All modifications are written to the transaction log before writing to the database. The transaction log provides a durable record of database activity and can be used for recovery purposes.

Transmission Control Protocol (TCP)   A transport layer protocol that implements guaranteed packet delivery using the Internet Protocol (IP).

Transmission Control Protocol/Internet Protocol (TCP/IP)   A suite of network protocols upon which the global Internet is based. TCP/IP is a general term that can refer either to the TCP and IP protocols used together or to the complete set of Internet protocols. TCP/IP is the default protocol for Windows NT.

Trigger   Triggers are event-oriented processes that start a stored procedure against an SQL database. A stored procedure is nothing more than a list of SQL statements. When you decide to make a change to an object in the site database through the SMS Administrator console, what happens behind the scenes is that a trigger fires off a stored procedure that makes the changes. Another kind of trigger can be set up to fire in Network Monitor when a certain event or threshold has occurred.

U

Uniform Resource Locator (URL)   An Internet standard naming convention for identifying resources available via various TCP/IP application protocols. For example, `http://www.microsoft.com` is the URL for Microsoft's World Wide Web server site, while `ftp://gateway.dec.com` is a popular FTP site. A URL allows easy hypertext references to a particular resource from within a document or mail message.

Universal Naming Convention (UNC)   A multi-vendor, multi-platform convention for identifying shared resources on a network. In the Microsoft world, you denote a UNC with double backslashes ("\\"), followed by the computer's NetBIOS name, another backslash, and then the share you'd like to connect to, e.g. `\\myserver\myshare`.

Unlicensed program   A software metering term, this is a software program that is neither a registered product nor an excluded program. You thus have the ability to monitor the usage of the product and then decide the approach you want to take about whether to monitor it via software metering.

User   In SQL Server, a database-specific identifier that maps to a login and allows access to database resources. If a user is mapped to a login entry in the SYSLogins system table of the server, that login is allowed access to the database and can access database objects. Users are stored in the SYSUsers system table of each database.

Username   A user's account name in a logon-authenticated system (like Windows NT and SQL Server).

V

View   In SQL Server, an object that is usually created to exclude certain columns from a table or to link two or more tables together. A view appears very much like a table to most users.

W

Web-based Enterprise Management (WBEM)   An initiative developed by the Distributed Management Task Force (DMTF) at www.dmtf.org. It is based on certain management and Internet technologies in order to unify the management of disparate enterprise computing environments.

Web browser   An application that makes HTTP requests and formats the resultant HTML documents for the users. The pre-eminent Internet client, most Web browsers understand all standard Internet protocols.

Web page   Any HTML document on an HTTP server.

Wildcard   The asterisk ("*") or question mark ("?") characters. Think of the asterisk as denoting the word "all." Think of the question mark as a placeholder for one character. You can use the asterisk wildcard in your SMS queries: e.g. Select * from *mytable* where username = "Fred". This query would return all columns and rows from the table *mytable* where the WHERE clause "username = 'FRED'" was a match. You can also use both wildcards in File Manager, Explorer, or at the command prompt: e.g. DIR my*.fi? would return a directory listing of all files beginning with the 2 letter string "MY" and also including any extension that has an "FI" as its first two letters. `myfiles.fil` and `mydog.fin` would both be a match on this wildcard search.

Win16   The set of application services provided by the 16-bit versions of Microsoft Windows: Windows 3.1 and Windows for Workgroups 3.11.

Win32   The set of application services provided by the 32-bit versions of Microsoft Windows: Windows 95/98 and Windows NT.

Windows 3.11 for Workgroups   The current 16-bit version of Windows for less-powerful, Intel-based personal computers; this system includes peer-networking services. Windows 3.1 was a predecessor to Windows 3.11.

Windows 95   The current 32-bit version of Microsoft Windows for medium-range, Intel-based personal computers; this system includes peer-networking services, Internet support, and strong support for older DOS applications and peripherals.

Windows 98   The latest version evolutionary version of Windows 95. Windows 98 includes over 3000 fixes from the original Windows 95 code, as well as tighter integration between the Internet and browsers and Windows 98.

Windows NT   The current 32-bit version of Microsoft Windows for powerful Intel, Alpha, PowerPC, or MIPS-based computers; the system includes peer-networking services, server-networking services, Internet client and server services, and a broad range of utilities. Windows NT Workstation is a version of Windows NT that is primarily used on desktop and laptop computers, but can act as a server for up to ten simultaneous connections at a time. Windows NT Server is a version of Windows NT that is primarily used as a file/application server that can theoretically have thousands of simultaneous users connected to it.

SQL Server 6.5 runs on either version (3.51 or 4) of Windows NT. SQL Server 7 requires Windows NT 4.

Windows NT Directory Replication   Windows NT has the ability to replicate files between folders. This feature is often used to replicate master copies of logon scripts to all the controllers in a domain.

Windows Management Instrumentation (WMI)   The Microsoft implementation for communicating with WBEM in order to retrieve collected management information from the SMS database. It uses client agent software, CIMOM, and other software componentry. WMI will become a more large-scale standard in use on Windows 98 and Windows 2000 for the wider goal of controlling the software/hardware instrumentation of Windows computer systems in general.

Workgroup   In Microsoft networks, a collection of related computers, such as a department, that don't require the uniform security and coordination of a domain. Workgroups are characterized by decentralized management as opposed to the centralized management that domains use. See also *Domain*.

World Wide Web (WWW)   A collection of Internet servers providing hypertext-formatted documents for Internet clients running Web browsers. The World Wide Web provided the first easy-to-use graphical interface for the Internet and is largely responsible for the Internet's explosive growth.

Y

Y2K (Year 2000)   Y2K refers to the problem that older computers and software have when handling years that end with 00, 01, etc. Many older systems didn't leave room for 4 digits in the year, just 2, which means that older systems may not function correctly in the year 2000. This usually shows up in the form of old COBOL code on mainframe computers, although PC and

Mid-size computing applications can exhibit this problem as well. The Y2K problem also includes what are termed *embedded systems*, microprocessor chips that perform one distinct function and are usually bundled with a device of some kind. Gas pumps would be a good example.

Z

Zulu A military and governmental reference to Greenwich mean time.

Index

Note to the Reader: Page numbers in **bold** indicate the principal discussion of a topic or the definition of a term. Page numbers in *italic* indicate illustrations.

C

I

K

L

M

Q

MCSE CORE EXAM NOTES™
FROM NETWORK PRESS®

TAKE YOUR CAREER TO THE NEXT LEVEL

with 24seven books from Network Press

- This new series offers the advanced information you need to keep your systems and networks running 24 hours a day, seven days a week.
- On-the-job case studies provide solutions to real-world problems.
- Maximize your system's uptime—and go home at 5!
- $34.99; 7½" x 9"; 544–704 pages; softcover

MCSE ELECTIVE STUDY GUIDES FROM NETWORK PRESS®

Sybex's Network Press expands the definitive Study Guide series for MCSE and MCSE+I candidates.